WAR IN THE PACIFIC

PACIFIC

1937–1945

WAR IN THE PACIFIC
1937–1945

Brompton

First published in 1991 by
Brompton Books Corp.
15 Sherwood Place
Greenwich, CT 06830

ISBN 0-86124-872-4

Printed in Hong Kong

PAGE 1: *The escort carrier* Gambier Bay *is bracketed by the splashes of Japanese shell fire during the crisis of the Battle of Leyte Gulf.*

PAGES 2-3: *Men of the 27th Marines on the beach at Iwo Jima.*

BELOW: *B-29 Superfortress bombers ready to take off from Tinian en route to Tokyo.*

CONTENTS

Introduction

Japan's popular image in the Western World has been colored, not to say damaged, by the propaganda of World War II. The comic strips and propaganda films produced during the war and immediately after which portrayed the Japanese as something less than human, buck-teethed, grinning demons who liked nothing better than to torture and kill Anglo-Saxons were hardly contradicted by the genuinely terrifying zeal of the kamikazes towards the end of the war. The rather apologetic subsequent attempts by Hollywood to rectify racist-inspired, wartime errors, as in Marlon Brando's screen versions of *Sayonara* and *The Teahouse of the August Moon* scarcely helped. Once the madman prepared to justify any act to serve his Emperor, the Japanese was now seen as the civilized creator of ornamental flower-arrangements, the appreciator of the moribund delicacy of the geisha or the contemplator of falling cherry blossoms. More recently, in the light of Japan's dramatic economic growth, the Japanese have been popularly viewed through the bifocals of admiration and jealousy as the super-efficient, globetrotting businessmen purveying Japanese-built television sets and automobiles with the missionary zeal of atonement for war crimes both real and imagined.

While all of these caricatures are as pathetic as they are absurd, like all cartoon figures, they contain more than a small measure of recognizable truth. As contradictory as each definition of the Japanese character may be, they almost disguise the fact that the Japanese people themselves are equally contradictory. The Japanese are a people wedded to the past as they chart and create the future. This dichotomy of alienation with the present as they test and surpass its boundaries has been a characteristic of the Japanese people ever since the decision was taken in the 1860s to absorb Western technology into the nation in order to prevent the destruc-tion of the essence of the Japanese national character (*kokutai*) through colonization, which appeared more than possible just over a hundred years ago. The heart of the problem lies in the fact that in becoming superficially Westernized the *kokutai* may be destroyed or permanently altered by the Japanese themselves. This contradiction, as important to understanding Japan today as it is to understanding the history of the past century, was never more present than in the course of the years before and during the Second World War.

The Japanese warrior tradition was a thousand years old when a group of samurai from the Provinces of Satsuma, Choshu, Hizen and Tosa conspired to overthrow the Tokugawa shogunate and establish the Emperor Meiji as *de facto* ruler of Japan in 1868. These samurai took this step when it became clear that, under the Shogunate, modernization, which could stave off Western invasion, would never take place. In the generation which followed the Meiji Restoration of 1868 Japan sought to create a modern industrial machine as well as a defense force which could ward off invasion from the West. Japan had seen how other oriental nations had been humiliated by Western arms – China, India, and the countries of Southeast Asia – and was unwilling to be dealt with in such a cursory manner. The first test came in the Sino-Japanese War of 1894-95. Although Japan won a stunning victory against a poorly-equipped and badly-organized Chinese Army and Navy, two facts became readily apparent to Japan's new masters: first, all the spoils of war could be stripped from them by a mere piece of paper, when Russia, France and Germany ordered Japan to remove her troops from territory recently won in the war, the strategically located Liaotung Peninsula in southern Manchuria. Secondly, Japan's military might could handle an Asian enemy, but was no match for a combination of Western forces which might

RIGHT: *A naval kamikaze pilot dons his ceremonial scarf prior to a mission.*

be ranged against her. Japan, it seemed, had no choice but to renew her efforts to build a modern army and navy and to look for a Western ally in order to accomplish this end.

Japan found her ally in Great Britain. With Germany arming, Britain wanted to withdraw forces from the Far East and elsewhere to strengthen her position closer to home, and signed the Anglo-Japanese alliance in 1902. This document permitted Japan to purchase military equipment of a high standard which at the time she was unable to produce in quantity herself. Although Japan had already placed orders for ships in British yards, the alliance placed her in a more favorable position to acquire weapons of war virtually on demand. When Japan avenged the humiliation of 1895 in the attack on Russian Port Arthur in the Liaotung Peninsula early in 1904, Japan took her first step on the road to world recognition as a major military power. It was the first step toward her involvement in World War II. While her victory over Russia stunned the world, Japan found herself at the end of the conflict with only one significant rival for hegemony in the Pacific: the United States. Japan as well had become the champion of Asian nationalism, since it was Japan which was the first country in Asia to defeat a Western power in modern times. Asian nationalists in China, Indonesia and India took heart at what had happened at Port Arthur and Tsushima. Japan's victory proved the West was not invulnerable. Racist claims of white superiority were disproved, and Japan saw herself as not only the leader of a pan-Asian attempt to rid the area of the Westerners: she saw herself as a world power ready to take her place as a world-class decision-maker equal to all and second to none.

The Western powers did not view Japan's victory in the same light. Britain tried unsuccessfully to dissuade Japan from entering World War I and was subjected to heavy criticism from Australia and New Zealand, for allowing Japan to seize so much territory from Germany in 1914-15. The capture of Shantung Province placed Japan in a powerful position in North China, but the acquisition of the Marshalls, Marianas and Carolines gave Japan dominance in the Western Pacific which threatened Australia's north coast. Her rapid victory did not escape the notice of the United States either, whose Philippine colony lay exposed to possible Japanese attack. But there was little the Anglophone nations could do. Japan was determined to create a sphere of influence in the Pacific and continued to build and rebuild a war machine to maintain and expand it.

Although the Western victors in World War I could not deny Japan the spoils of her easy conquests at the Paris Peace Conference in 1919, they did try to limit Japanese naval expansion at the Washington Conference of 1921-22. On balance the terms were not unreasonable, but within a Japanese context it was difficult to justify either to the voters or to the growing military machine the fact that Japan was still being treated as an inferior. While this was not of primary importance during the 1920s when business, particularly with the US, was good, it quickly became of vital importance when the Depression began in 1930. Japan, as a recently industrialized state, was hit first and hardest by the slump in America which soon became worldwide. Since Chiang Kai-shek's China was already encroaching on Japan's sphere of influence in Manchuria, it was inevitable that someone would take action. In the event, it was the Japanese Army which acted alone in seizing the whole of Manchuria in 1931. From this point on the position of civilian government in Japan began to crumble. The Army and the Navy vied for influence with the government, the industrial barons and the Emperor. Greater incursions were made in China and government by assassination became the rule of the day.

ABOVE: *The British battlecruiser* Repulse, *sent to Malaysian waters late in 1941 to deter Japan from going to war. Instead she and her consort* Prince of Wales *were quickly sunk by Japanese aircraft.*

Was there any way for the West to mitigate these steps which can now be seen to have led Japan down the road to authoritarian government, war with the West, and inevitable defeat? Certainly the West could have been less hypocritical in allowing Japan a tangible sphere of influence in China. But even this would not have appeased the leaders of an ever-powerful Japanese war machine, striving to achieve hegemony at home and dominance abroad. Japan was diplomatically isolated in an increasingly dangerous world in the 1930s. Her industrial development, still in a formative stage, demanded a secure market and source of raw materials in a world economic crisis. Led by men whose training and upbringing echoed the warrior code of Bushido transmitted to them from scores of generations of samurai administrators. Japan, in her search for security, could not fail to turn to those who were prepared to find international security in a decisive way. It was the only way they knew: the way of the warrior.

Yet, because of her still slender industrial base, Japan could not hope to wage war and win it on her own. Japan's conquest of China was as easy as it was brutal in its early stages, but in order to achieve final victory, if final victory over a nation like China was ever possible, Japan

needed raw materials which still lay in Western hands. The choice was retreat and humiliation, or bold attack. To a warrior, defeat with honor was preferable, and to Japan's leaders defeat was by no means certain. If victory was attainable, the opportunity of a millenium had to be taken. When Japan took on the West at Pearl Harbor, the honorable, heroic and disastrous decision was made.

The contradictions of Japan's rapid rise to world power became all too evident in the four years of World War II in the Pacific. In China Japan was already stretched to its limits; after Pearl Harbor it reached the breaking point. The amazing resilience of the Japanese people and their continual inventiveness kept the war effort going. The courage and tenacity of her fighting men compensated for the lack of pilots, planes and ships when Japan's industrial capacity broke down under the dual pressures of Allied bombing and fundamental weakness. Nevertheless Japan held off the world's most powerful industrial nation for four years. She dominated Southeast Asia and China as no modern nation has ever done. Her ferocity in battle and courage in the face of disaster were second to none in what was to become greatest war that the world has ever known.

1.
The Road to
Pearl Harbor

On the night of 18 September 1931, a Japanese patrol engaged a small Chinese force in a firefight near Mukden following the investigation of explosions in the area which had slightly damaged a railway line leading into the city. The next morning, units of Japan's Kwantung Army occupied Mukden, Changchun, and laid siege to the city of Kirin which fell two days later. The Manchurian Incident had begun.

In retrospect, it is clear that the minor clash which occurred between Japanese and Chinese forces on the night of 18 September was a rather flimsy pretext for what quickly developed to become a full-scale invasion of Manchuria. Under normal circumstances, such a fracas would probably never have been reported. However, normal circumstances did not prevail at the time. Commanders of the Kwantung Army, Japan's crack force in Manchuria, had long hoped for the opportunity to engage Chinese forces in the area and their army had been placed on alert at least three days prior to the incident of the 18th, suggesting that what occurred in Manchuria after September 1931 was hardly a spontaneous response to a local crisis. On the contrary, it was a cold and calculated gesture, taken without prior notification and/or approval from the government in Tokyo.

By the time that the news of the situation in Manchuria reached Tokyo, reinforcements had been sent to Manchuria from Korea and the Japanese Cabinet was faced with a *fait accompli*. Try as they might, government leaders found themselves powerless to halt the advance of Japanese forces in Manchuria since field commanders simply ignored their orders, arguing that local conditions produced operational necessities which required action contrary to orders from Tokyo. Furthermore, field commanders in Manchuria were supported by the General Staff and the War Ministry.

The invasion of Manchuria was a bad omen of things to come. Japanese forces successfully completed their occupation of the area by the end of the year in spite of decisions made in Tokyo. Put in other words, the Manchurian Incident inaugurated a series of episodes in which decisions which vitally affected the course of Japanese history and diplomacy were made by army officers in the field while the government in Tokyo stood by powerless to act except in response to *faits accomplis*.

By January 1932 hostilities in Manchuria were concluded but the *de facto* war between the Chinese and Japanese continued, spilling over into China proper where rival forces clashed in Shanghai and Nanking. Powerless to protect their interests by force, the Chinese appealed to the League of Nations, hoping for some kind of action to stop Japan's advance and return Manchuria to Chinese control. Responding to this appeal, the League appointed an investigatory committee headed by Lord Lytton of Great Britain. This investigation was initially approved by the Japanese government which publicly denied China's charges of aggression but privately hoped that the force of world opinion might have a restraining influence on ambitious officers in the Imperial Army.

If some political leaders in the Diet hoped that League of Nations' intervention would put a damper on further incursions of the Imperial Army into the realm of foreign policy, they were mistaken. In March 1932, even as the Lytton Commission was conducting its investigation, Pu Yi, the last Emperor of the Ch'ing (Manchu)

ABOVE: *Emperor Hirohito of Japan.*

LEFT: *Japanese troops celebrate as their easy early victories begin to unfold.*

RIGHT: *Prince Konoye and members of the Japanese Cabinet in 1937. Konoye was also Prime Minister for much of 1940-41 but was replaced by the more militant General Tojo in October 1941.*

dynasty, was brought back from obscurity and placed on the throne of the new state, Manchukuo, created by military fiat. This ended the possibility that the Lytton Commission might succeed and ultimately resulted in the first major crisis faced by the League of Nations.

As might have been expected, the report of the Lytton Commission was highly critical of Japanese activities in Manchuria. The report, which was submitted to the League in September 1932, condemned Japan and called for a voluntary Japanese withdrawal from all areas occupied by force in Manchuria. Since such a suggestion was totally unacceptable to the Imperial Army and the general public, the Japanese government had little choice but to denounce the Lytton Report and withdraw from the League of Nations in February 1933. Whatever reservations member of the Cabinet and Diet may have had about the whole affair, they dared not criticize the military for fear of their lives as well as their careers.

Although the international ramifications of the Manchurian Incident were serious, domestic political repercussions were even more critical. The Wakatsukii government was forced to resign in December 1931, following which a series of successors grappled with the constitutional crisis posed by military activities in Manchuria. Making matters even more ominous for Japan's civilian political leaders was the rash of violence and assassination plots launched by political radicals following the Manchurian Incident. Between February and May 1932 at least three major political figures were assassinated, including Prime Minister Inukai who was shot in his official residence. These terror tactics did not succeed in laying the ground work for an immediate military *coup d'état* as their perpetrators may have wished but they bode ill for the continuation of a viable parliamentary system in Japan.

The assassins of Prime Minister Inukai were brought to trial in the summer of 1933, but rather than being condemned by the public and the court, they were lauded as patriots. Their trial became a focus for expounding patriotic doctrines in defense of Japanese expansion on the continent. To foreign observers, it appeared as if it was the government and not the assassins who were on trial and the sentences handed down by the court seemed to confirm this view. Of the men involved in Inukai's murder and other assassination attempts, only one received a long jail sentence. The others received little more than token sentences or verbal reprimands. Such leniency by the courts could hardly have en-

ABOVE: *Japanese troops move into Nanking in December 1937. This peaceful scene belies the reality that the Japanese soldiers carried out a rampage of rape and murder in the town.*

ABOVE LEFT: *A Russian prisoner of the Japanese during their clash in 1939.*

LEFT: *The US gunboat* Panay *was attacked and sunk by the Japanese on the Yangtze on 12 December 1937.*

couraged party leaders in the Diet and those who opposed the trend of events. Members of patriotic societies, on the other hand, were buoyed up by the court's decision and continued their brazen attacks on the political system.

One immediate result of the Manchurian Incident and subsequent domestic violence was the end of effective party government. Discouraged and frightened by what was happening, leaders of the major political parties feared to take strong stands in opposition to the military. Furthermore, they found it impossible to form viable governments given the unwillingness of the Army and Navy to participate in the Cabinet by releasing men from active service to serve as Ministers of the Army and Navy. As a result, it was necessary to resort to the device of coalition Cabinets headed by non-party men acceptable to extremists in the military. Indeed, the two men who followed Inukai as prime ministers were

both admirals, their choice based upon the assumption of the party men that they would be easier to control than more radical types in the Imperial Army. Unfortunately, the party men were naive in their assumption that such a compromise would buy time to restore civilian control of the government.

Japanese expansion on the mainland continued in 1933. Undaunted by the League of Nations censure, the worsening of Japanese-American relations, and the continuation of political agitation at home, the Kwantung Army added the province of Jehol to the Kingdom of Manchukuo at the beginning of the year. In May a demilitarized buffer zone south of Manchuria was created as a result of the Tangku Truce with China, a pact negotiated by military men and not the Foreign Ministry. Compared to the dramatic territorial gains of 1931 and 1932, these advances were on a small scale but still represented a con-

tinued usurpation of power by the military. Such a situation continued to prevail in the years that followed when the provinces of Hopei and Chahar in China fell victim to Japanese control. As 1936 dawned, the Imperial Army was well on its way to making China a Japanese protectorate.

By the beginning of 1936 the question of who controlled the Japanese government, the party men or the military, had been resolved in favor of the military. Another question, however, remained to be answered. That was which faction controlled the military, particularly the Imperial Army. Just as the Diet was divided into two major parties plus various factional groups, so too was the Army divided. One group, the Imperial Way faction or Kodo, called for continued expansion in Manchuria and a more aggressive stance *vis-à-vis* the Diet. Another group, the Control or Tosei faction, was more concerned with the situation in China and seemingly preferred to work within the existing political system to effect

LEFT: *A bomb explodes above the target ship during the so-called Mitchell Tests conducted by the Americans in 1923. Although the test conditions were highly artificial, they did much to advance the cause of naval air power.*

BELOW: *President Roosevelt broadcasting in September 1940.*

change. Members of these factions also differed with regard to the definition of Japan's enemies, the Kodo faction seeing the Soviet Union as Japan's primary adversary while the Tosei clique viewed China as Japan's principal enemy, at least for the moment. Both groups, however, shared the view that the Japanese government should pursue a positive foreign policy which called for continued expansion of Japanese interests on the continent.

During 1935 and 1936 the Kodo and Tosei factions waged an internal war for control of the Imperial Army. At first the Kodo faction enjoyed a more favorable position, its leaders Generals Araki and Mazaki serving as Minister of War and Director-General of Military Education respec-

tively. In 1935, however, Tosei advocates were seriously threatening Kodo dominance. When General Nagata, leader of the Tosei clique, secured the dismissal of General Mazaki in July 1935, the quiet political battle for control of the Imperial Army became violent.

On 12 August 1935 General Nagata was assassinated by a young officer of the Kodo faction. When the assassin was court-martialed and tried for murder, Kodo adherents once again resorted to force. On the morning of 26 February 1936, approximately one thousand troops of the First Division which guarded Tokyo and was commanded by Kodo supporters attempted to take over the city, attacking the residences of the Prime Minister and other government officials.

ABOVE RIGHT: *Prime Minister Churchill visited the US for talks immediately after Pearl Harbor. He is shown addressing the US Congress on 26 December 1941.*

LEFT: *The Japanese battleship* Nagato *like all the major Japanese vessels, was extensively updated during the years before WW2.*

Although the Prime Minister was not killed this time, many others were, including the Finance Minister, the Lord Privy Seal, and the new Director-General of Military Education.

The attempted *coup d'état* was aborted on 29 February when the Imperial Guards and selected units of the Imperial Navy were called to Tokyo. Taking unusually prompt and decisive action, government leaders arrested and tried the leaders of the ill-fated rebellion, thirteen of whom were executed. Unlike the show trials of 1932, the defendants were not permitted to use the courtroom as a soap-box for the propagation of ultra-nationalism. Furthermore, even those leaders of the Kodo faction not directly involved in the affair of 26 February were punished, Generals Araki and Mazaki being retired from active service and placed on reserve. Other officers remained on active service but were transferred to 'safe' posts.

Although discipline was returned to the Imperial Army, a dear price was paid for the restoration of order. The new leaders of the Army, almost all members of the Tosei faction, demanded a free hand in matters relating to China as a reward for their suppression of the Kodo revolt and forced the government to accede to their demands by refusing to participate in the Cabinet unless given *carte blanche* in questions relating to national security. Since no Cabinet could function without a Minister of War, military leaders were able to exercise a *de facto* veto over government decisions to an extent hitherto unknown.

With the Tosei faction safely ensconced in the War Ministry, it was only a matter of time before renewed Sino-Japanese hostilities became a reality. The wait was short. In July 1937 a clash between Chinese and Japanese troops near Peking provided the rationale for yet another expansion of Japanese interests in China. The Marco Polo Bridge Incident was a relatively minor one, but Japanese commanders did not need much of an excuse to renew hostilities with the Chinese. Once again, despite the reluctance of the government to use the Marco Polo Bridge Incident as a pretext for a full-scale confrontation with Chiang Kai-shek, local commanders dictated what action was to be taken, plunging

BELOW: *The US Fleet base at Pearl Harbor photographed in October 1941, much as it would have appeared to the first attacking Japanese aircraft. Unlike a few weeks later, however, an aircraft carrier berthed by Ford Island is among the ships in port.*

ABOVE: *The destroyer Ward was the first American unit in action against the Japanese when it attacked a Japanese midget submarine early on 7 December.*

RIGHT: *Admiral Yamamoto, planner of the attack on Pearl Harbor.*

Japan into a long and costly struggle in China.

Within a month after the initial encounter between Chinese and Japanese forces at the Marco Polo Bridge on 7 July 1937, Japanese troops had successfully occupied Peking and Tientsin. By the beginning of September over 150,000 Japanese troops were stationed in China. What is more important, they were being moved south to confront Chinese Nationalist armies defending Shanghai and Nanking. The battles for Shanghai and Nanking were hard-fought contests with Chinese forces putting up fierce resistance to Japanese troops for the first time in modern history. Eventually, such resistance failed, Shanghai and Nanking falling to the Japanese by the year's end.

Unaccustomed to resistance from Chinese armies, the Japanese sustained very heavy casualties in their quest for Shanghai and Nanking and retaliated by going on a rampage of death, destruction, pillage, and rape after taking these cites, particularly Nanking. Such behaviour was widely criticized in the West. More important, it seemed to fortify Chiang Kaishek's will to resist. Thus, Japanese efforts to negotiate a settlement with the Chinese fell on deaf ears in 1937 and 1938. This fact pleased some Japanese commanders who grew less interested in a negotiated settlement of the China Incident as Japanese victories continued. They demanded nothing less than the total capitulation of the Chinese including the resignation of Chiang Kai-shek as preconditions for ending hostilities in China. Needless to say, given this set of preconditions, serious negotiations were impossible.

In 1938 Japanese forces continued their advance in China, forcing the Chinese to evacuate the major urban centers along the Yangtze River as well as all coastal ports from Shanghai south to Canton. With the exception of the provinces of Szechwan and Yunnan, most of China proper was in Japanese hands. Despite this fact, Chiang Kai-shek's government refused to capitulate to the Japanese, thus posing economic and political problems for the Imperial Army. Although the China Incident had dragged on longer than had originally been anticipated, the full resources of the Japanese had not been marshalled to secure a military victory. As one observer pointed out at the time, the war in China was more nearly akin to a colonial war of attrition

than to a total war. Nevertheless, the longer the China Incident dragged on without result, the more war weary the Japanese became. Furthermore, if the military effort was to be continued, the domestic economy would be subject to increased strain. Whether the Japanese people would accept such a situation without protest remained questionable.

Fearing that further extension of the conflict in China would have adverse effects at home, Japanese leaders re-evaluated the situation in China in 1939, ultimately deciding to abandon further military offensives in favor of a policy of consolidation and cooperation with various puppet regimes in occupied China. At the same time, the Japanese launched a diplomatic effort to isolate the regime of Chiang Kai-shek by closing supply routes into free China from Burma and Indochina, thereby making it impossible for the Chinese Nationalists to continue their resistance.

After 1938 there were only two routes over which supplies could be carried into free China. The first was through the port of Haiphong and over the Haiphong-Hanoi-Yunnan railway line.

ABOVE: *A Japanese Kate torpedo bomber, one of the trio of aircraft which made up the Pearl Harbor attack force. This example is shown under test in the US in 1943 after being captured.*

LEFT: *Cheering crewmembers on a Japanese carrier watch one of their air group take off, dawn, 7 December 1941.*

RIGHT: *A flight deck officer aboard a Japanese carrier watches the attack begin.*

The second was through the port of Rangoon and over the Burma Road, an even more circuitous and difficult route. If the Japanese could persuade the British and French to close these access routes, China would surely capitulate.

Japanese diplomats pressed their case with the British and French in 1939 and 1940. At the same time, less subtle pressures were exerted. In February 1939 Japanese forces occupied Hainan Island, a French interest, off the China coast. Three months later, Japanese forces briefly blockaded the British and French concessions in Tientsin. If these acts were not sufficient to persuade the European powers to accede to Japan's

demands, the outbreak of war in Europe in September provided a more compelling reason to do so. By the end of 1940 both the British and Vichy French governments had agreed to close the ports of Rangoon and Haiphong to goods bound for free China. At year's end, it looked as if victory was in sight.

With the prospect of continued Chinese resistance hopefully eliminated as a result of Japan's arrangement with the British and the French, the Japanese government and military were seemingly free to turn their attention to the Soviet threat in the north. Clashes between Japanese and Russian forces along their long

ABOVE: *Douglas SBD Dauntless dive bombers in flight over the carrier* Enterprise *in October 1941. The Dauntless would eventually sink more Japanese shipping than any other Allied aircraft.*

RIGHT: *An early model Mitsubishi Zero. The high performance of the Zero came as a considerable shock to the Allies in the early months of the war.*

BELOW: *Zeros warming up aboard a Japanese carrier preparatory to taking off for Pearl Harbor.*

海軍省許可済第七八三號

common border north of Manchuria had occurred with increased frequency in 1938 and 1939, causing great concern in Tokyo since the Japanese had not fared well.

Fear of the Soviets led the Japanese to reconsider their relationship with Hitler and the German government. The Anti-Comintern Pact which the Japanese had signed with Germany in November 1936 provided a defensive alliance against Russia under certain limited circumstances plus a rather meaningless pledge against the spread of Communism. Since neither of these provisions provided much assurance of German intervention in the event of a war between Japan and the Soviet Union, many officers in the Imperial Army urged the negotiation of a bilateral defense pact which would provide insurance against a Russian attack. Accordingly, the Japanese Ambassador in Berlin, General Oshima Hiroshi, was instructed to initiate discussions with the German government in June 1938.

Preliminary Japanese-German talks got nowhere. The Germans showed little interest in the idea of a bilateral agreement, preferring a broader accord involving others, particularly the Italians. The Japanese government balked at this, but talks were continued. However, with the announcement of the Nazi-Soviet Pact in August 1939, talks were quickly broken off not to be resumed until after the outbreak of war in Europe.

Although disappointed by the failure of the initial Japanese-German negotiations, Japanese leaders continued to lean toward a German alliance. Germany's early victories over Poland, Belgium, the Netherlands, and France only served to strengthen this view. Furthermore, the need for some kind of agreement with Hitler seemed even more pressing, considering the opportunity for expansion into the Southeast Asian colonies of France and Holland which had been so recently defeated by the Germans. The Japanese were very much interested in the mineral resources of the area but before they made any move, they had to know the intention of the Reich *vis-à-vis* these colonies. Thus, in July 1940, the Japanese re-opened discussions.

ABOVE: *A Japanese torpedo strikes home on the battleship* West Virginia *as the Pacific Fleet begins to pay for its lack of preparedness.*

ABOVE: *The ammunition magazine of the destroyer* Shaw *explodes during the Pearl Harbor attack.*

OVERLEAF: *Rescue and firefighting vessels alongside the damaged* West Virginia.

Under the watchful eye of Japan's new Foreign Minister, Matsuoka Yosuke, Japanese-German negotiations proceeded rapidly, culminating in the signing of the Tripartite Pact with Germany and Italy on 27 September 1940. With the signing of this agreement, the Japanese turned their attention to the Soviet problem. Convinced that a war with the Russians would be a disaster, the Foreign Ministry initiated discussions with the Soviets which led to the conclusion of a Russo-Japanese Neutrality Agreement in April 1941. The signing of this agreement with the Soviets ended the immediate prospect of a war in Manchuria and permitted the government to take advantage of the power vacuum in Southeast Asia created by the preoccupation of the colonial powers with Europe.

The idea of Japanese military expansion into Southeast Asia was not a new one. It had been discussed by military leaders throughout the 1930's. The rich reserves of oil, tin, rubber, bauxite, and rice known to exist in the region made it increasingly attractive to military men who were only too keenly aware of Japan's

dependency on imports of such items from the United States and other sources. As long as Japan remained dependent upon such imports in large quantities, she would be vulnerable to blackmail by those who controlled the supply of such vital prerequisites for modern industry. Although this fact did not seem to bother Japanese business leaders, many senior officers were obsessed by the matter. Thus, when war broke out in Europe, considerable pressure was put on the government to take advantage of the situation to acquire more direct access to vital resources by seizing the colonies of the European powers.

On 27 July 1940 the question of expansion of Japan's interest in Southeast Asia was raised at an Imperial Liaison Conference. It was decided at that time to take advantage of the preoccupation of the powers with the war by initiating discussions with these powers and their colonial governments with an eye towards increasing the quotas of vital raw materials shipped to Japan from these colonies. Although the conference did not approve military preparations for a move

south, it was clear that if diplomatic efforts failed, force would follow.

The Foreign Ministry lost no time in implementing the decision of the Liaison Conference. In August 1940 Japanese and French diplomats began talks which resulted in an agreement in September permitting the Japanese to establish military and naval installations in Tonkin and to move troops through Indochina in the event of war with another power. In return for these concessions, the Japanese promised to continue to recognize French sovereignty in Indochina. Negotiations with Dutch colonial officials in the Indies proved less fruitful. Despite their even more precarious position than the French, Dutch officials in Batavia refused to accept Japan's demand for special economic and political privileges in the Islands, leaving the impression in Tokyo that only the use of force would provide Japan with all of the oil she needed from the Dutch.

Discussion of Japanese expansion into Southeast Asia was based upon pragmatic considerations but also fit neatly into the ideological rationalizations for such expansion on the continent, *e.g.* the concept of a New Order in East Asia. As originally envisaged by Prime Minister Konoye in 1938, this New Order would link Japan, Korea, China and Manchuria in an economic and political commonwealth dominated by Japan. Such a pan-Asian ideal could easily be expanded to include the colonies and states of Southeast Asia and this was what was suggested by Japanese propagandists in 1940 when they called for the creation of a Greater East Asia Co-Prosperity Sphere in place of the New Order. If anything, the idea of the Co-Prosperity Sphere was even more attractive than the earlier call for the creation of a New Order in East Asia because of the economic potential of this larger unit. Furthermore, it would be relatively easy to add the Southeast Asian colonies to Japan's orbit, given the preoccupation of the powers with the European war and the anti-colonial prejudices of the people of the region.

The concept of the Greater East Asia Co-Prosperity Sphere found considerable support among the military, in the government, and among the general population. The most ardent proponents of the Co-Prosperity Sphere called for immediate and vigorous action to realize their dream, pointing out that the British, Dutch, and French were in no position to halt Japan's advance. Had it not been for the fact that the United Sates remained aloof from the war and in a position to oppose further Japanese expansion, the Japanese expansionists might have had their

way in 1940. Such, however, was not to be the case.

As of 1940, Japanese leaders were unwilling to risk a war with the United States as the price for southward expansion, at least not until the position of the American government relative to Japan's new role in Asia was clarified. Although it was no secret that the Americans opposed Japan's occupation of China after 1937 in a manner consistent with their earlier response to the Manchurian Incident, the United States had taken no action to break off diplomatic relations with Japan nor to impose economic sanctions of an effective nature. On the other hand, the Japanese could not assume that this would continue to be the case in the future. Indeed, there were tell-tale signs that such action might be taken in the event of a Japanese occupation of the Southeast Asian colonies of the European powers. In 1939, for example, the United States refused to discuss renewal of the Japanese-American Treaty of Commerce which was due to expire in 1940. Furthermore, in the face of mounting opposition to Japanese expansion, the Roosevelt administration inaugurated a licensing system for exports of vital materials to Japan in 1940. Although Roosevelt did not immediately choose to embargo exports to Japan, he was eventually forced to do so, placing a ban on the export of all scrap metals in September and adding to the embargo list after his re-election.

Given the fact that American firms supplied Japan with at least 65 percent of her petroleum imports, which as of January 1941 were not on the embargo list, Japanese leaders sought to obtain a diplomatic agreement relative to their New Order before resorting to force. Their occupation of southern Indochina later that year led President Roosevelt to freeze all Japanese assets in the United States, bringing trade between Japan and the United States to a halt, much to the horror of many Japanese. This action, more than any other, convinced Japanese leaders of the resolve of the American government and the need to make one last effort at a negotiated settlement with the United States. Accordingly, Japan's new Ambassador to the United States, Admiral Nomura Kichisaburo, was instructed to open up a dialogue with Secretary of State Cordell Hull.

Ambassador Nomura was a well-known proponent of Japanese-American rapprochement. His appointment was designed to reassure the United Sates of Japan's desire for peaceful solutions in Asia and to provide a climate in which meaningful negotiations might take place. Before leaving Tokyo, Nomura had been in-

structed to inform Hull and Roosevelt that Japan was ready to renounce further use of force in Asia if the United States moved to restore normal economic relations with Japan and served as an intermediary in arranging peace talks with the Chinese Nationalists. This message was conveyed in the first round of conversations between Nomura and Hull.

American response to Nomura's message was cool, Secretary of State Hull suggesting that before progress could be made in resolving Japanese-American differences, the Japanese would have to recognize four basic principles, these being: 1) respect for the territorial integrity and sovereignty of all states in Asia; 2) a promise not to interfere in the internal affairs of any Asian state; 3) acceptance of the Open Door principle; 4) renunciation of the use of force to achieve economic and/or political ends.

Hull's response to Nomura's initiative was unacceptable to the Japanese. If accepted, Hull's preconditions would have meant a renunciation of all Japanese activities since 1931 and a withdrawal of Japanese forces from Manchuria, China and Indochina. No government could long survive in Tokyo if it accepted such terms. On the other hand, the Japanese were not ready to give up the idea of a diplomatic settlement with the United States. Thus, Japanese-American talks continued throughout 1941. In the meanwhile, plans for war were prepared and discussed.

In preparing for war with the United States, two considerations were primary, weather conditions and Japan's stockpile of vital commodi-

ties. Given the limitation of resources at their disposal, the Japanese could not endure a prolonged war nor could they expect a total victory over the combined might of the United States, the United Kingdom, and the Netherlands. What was called for was a limited pre-emptive strike designed to neutralize the Pacific Fleet of the United States at Pearl Harbor while Japanese forces simultaneously invaded Burma, the Dutch East Indies, Malaya, and the Philippines. Once this was achieved, it was assumed that a permanent diplomatic settlement with the USA and the other powers would follow.

If economic realities dictated a limited war to neutralize American forces in the Pacific, weather conditions necessitated that action be taken no later than the beginning of December 1941. This was reported to the Supreme War Council in Tokyo on 6 September 1941, at which time preliminary plans for the simultaneous attacks on Pearl Harbor and Southeast Asia were

presented and discussed. These plans were accepted at that time, and war games off the Japanese coast commenced later that month.

As preparations for war continued, Prime Minister Konoye was forced to resign, being replaced by General Tojo Hideki on 18 October 1941. Tojo's rise to power eliminated what little influence party men exercised within the government and facilitated the effort to mobilize the country for war with the United States. While such mobilization went on, however, one last effort at diplomacy was tried with the dispatch of the Kurusu mission to the United States.

The Kurusu mission had little chance of success since the Tojo government was unwilling to make any concessions beyond those originally offered by Ambassador Nomura several months before. As might have been expected, Secretary of State Hull rejected Kurusu's program but not before several weeks had elapsed during which both sides completed last minute preparations for war. Five days after Hull formally rejected Kurusu's last offer on 26 November 1941, the Imperial War Council in Tokyo ordered plans for the attack on Pearl Harbor to proceed. The point of no return had been reached.

Plans for a general Japanese offensive had been laid down long before 1941. They owed their origin to a National Defense Policy, formulated as early 1909. This, for the purposes of fleet

ABOVE: *The battleship* Nevada *did manage to get under way during the Japanese attack but was ordered to be run ashore when it was feared she might sink in the main entrance channel to the harbor.*

RIGHT: *In dock when the Japanese attacked were the destroyers* Cassin *and* Downes *and the battleship* Pennsylvania. *The Japanese failed to bomb other port facilities, however.*

maneuvers, had stipulated the United States as a purely hypothetical enemy, but had increased in relevance as the century progressed. It centered upon the assumption that the Americans would take the offensive in the Western Pacific – that is, virtually in Japanese home waters – as soon as hostilities began, and planned the destruction of the US fleet somewhere between the Marianas and Marshall Islands. In other words, the Americans would sail straight into a carefully-laid trap. But things had changed since 1909, particularly so far as Japanese aspirations were concerned, and by the late 1930s revisions were desperately needed. They were provided by Admiral Yamamoto Isoroku.

Appointed Commander in Chief of the Japanese Combined Fleet on 30 August 1939, Yamamoto recognized immediately that existing

war plans were unsatisfactory. They were based upon a defensive stance, waiting for the Americans to appear, whereas if hostilities began the exact opposite was intended, with a southward thrust to gain the Dutch East Indies and their essential oil fields before the British, Dutch and Americans could react. This necessitated a concentration of Japanese naval and military power away from the area of intended fleet action, leaving the route to Japan itself dangerously exposed, particularly as the Americans, in May 1940, had moved their Pacific Fleet from the West Coast to Pearl Harbor in the Central Pacific island of Oahu, a part of the Hawaiian chain. A westward thrust by this fleet could be decisive, threatening Japan and cutting the vulnerable lines of communication with forces attacking the Dutch East Indies. This led Yamamoto to the conclusion that if war was inevitable, the first Japanese action should be an attack upon Pearl Harbor to destroy the US Pacific fleet at its base. He began to work for this from the start of his command.

At first he had to tread carefully in the face of entrenched opposition from the Naval General Staff, gradually pushing the area of intended fleet action eastward until it included the waters around Hawaii. This was accepted in principle, but as the main part of the Japanese fleet was already earmarked for the protection of the southward push, it seemed, a hollow victory. It was then that Yamamoto introduced his trump card – the use of naval aircraft, taking off from a carrier force stationed near Hawaii, to bomb the Americans in a surprise attack. The idea was revolutionary and immediately opposed, but Yamamoto was convinced of its viability. He had always been interested in the capabilities of air power, recognizing it as a crucial new element of naval strategy as early as 1927, and when he was appointed to the aircraft carrier *Akagi* in 1928 he had devoted himself to the practical problems involved in the developing theories of air warfare. By 1937 he was sure in his own mind that attacks by torpedo-carrying aircraft could destroy any battleship then afloat, and that the key to naval supremacy in the future lay with the aircraft carrier and its long-range strike potential. If a force of carriers could approach Hawaii in secret, the war could commence with a powerful aerial strike upon the US fleet in Pearl Harbor, destroying battleships and shore installations to a crippling extent.

Preparations for such an assault began in late 1939, well before the Naval General Staff had given its blessing, with Yamamoto insisting upon a high standard of proficiency in carrier-based attacks throughout the naval air arm. In addition he managed to persuade his superiors to increase the carrier-building program and to authorize the introduction of new naval aircraft. By the end of 1940 Japan was well stocked in both respects. Four carriers – the *Akagi, Kaga, Hiryu* and *Soryu* – were immediately available, with two others – the *Shokaku* and *Zuikaku* – expected to be ready by August 1941; long-range flying boats, capable of carrying 2000-pound bomb loads over 800 miles had been introduced into service, and a new fighter aircraft, the A6M Zero, had been put into production. A reliable torpedo bomber, the Nakajima B5N2 (later code named Kate by the Allies), already existed, while the Aichi D3A1 (Val) dive bomber, although approaching obsolescence, was still an adequate machine, capable of inflicting the necessary degree of damage. Taken together, equipment was clearly no problem, but Yamamoto had to gain permission to mount his *coup de main.*

Approaching the problem cautiously, he began by building up support from among his own staff, confiding firstly in his Chief of Staff Admiral Fukudome Shigeru and then in Rear Admiral Onishi Takajiro, Chief of Staff of the land-based 11th Air Fleet. It was the latter who introduced Yamamoto to Commander Genda Minoru, a brilliant and experienced naval airman, and it was at this point that the plan started to assume its final form. After ten days of careful study, Genda came to the conclusion that the projected operation was 'difficult but not impossible,' provided that certain changes were made. To begin with, he did not agree with Yamamoto that the main target should be the American battleships, preferring to aim for the destruction of carriers, particularly as three such vessels – the *Enterprise, Lexington* and *Saratoga* – were known to be with the Pacific Fleet. Similarly, he favored far more concentration of force than Yamamoto had envisaged, with all six Japanese carriers taking part, their aircraft making more than one attack if circumstances allowed. Onishi passed these comments on to the Commander in Chief, and Genda was requested to draw up a detailed plan.

This began to take shape toward the end of March 1941 under the code name Operation Z, with Genda gradually expanding the scope of the attack. According to his ideas, a special task force of twenty I-class submarines and five two-man midget submarines would approach Hawaii before war was declared, the former stationing themselves around Oahu to catch any American ships that tried to escape, with the latter actually entering Pearl Harbor to add to the chaos caused by the aerial strike. Meanwhile the main force of six carriers, protected by destroyers and cruisers, would take a circuitous route, well away from known shipping lanes, and approach Hawaii from the north, where least expected. A total of 360 aircraft, comprising torpedo bombers, high-level bombers and fighters, would be launched about 230 miles from Oahu, to arrive over Pearl Harbor just after dawn, preferably on a Sunday when the American fleet, following peace-time training routines, would be in harbor with only skeleton screws on board. Once over the anchorage, if surprise was complete the torpedo bombers would attack first, followed closely by the high-level bombers and then the dive bombers, with the fighters providing a protective air umbrella. If surprise had been lost, the fighters would go in first to gain control of the air over the targets, clearing the way for the bombers. Either way, the assaults, to be delivered by two waves of aircraft, would be expected to last no more than two hours all told.

Yamamoto accepted this scheme without reservation, organizing training schedules and making sure that technical problems were solved on time. After sailing round the coast of Japan to find a suitable training area, he chose Kagoshima Bay, south of Kyushu, a spot which bore a striking resemblance to Pearl Harbor, and it was here that his naval pilots, as yet unaware of their projected task, practiced the necessary skills. They quickly attained a very high standard, with dive bombers reducing their release-point to 1500 feet and high-level bombers achieving 80 percent accuracy against stationary targets. At the same time existing torpedoes were modified to take account of the shallow nature of Pearl Harbor (it was only 40 feet deep) and special bombs, capable of cutting through the armor plate of battleships, were introduced. By late October 1941, each pilot, in a series of special briefings on board the *Akagi*, had been assigned to individual targets; Commander Fuchida Mitsuo, an experienced air leader, had been chosen to command the air attack on the day; and the entire force had been placed under Rear Admiral Nagumo Chuichi. All that was missing was permission to go ahead.

This came eventually on 3 November, when Yamamoto and his entire staff threatened to resign unless a decision was made. Even then, there was a continuing possibility of a last-minute cancellation, for the Japanese Emperor was determined to continue diplomatic negotiations with the Americans for as long as possible, in the hope that some kind of compromise could be worked out to prevent his militaristic govern-

RIGHT: *A Japanese photo of Battleship Row at the height of the attack.*

BELOW: *Rescue and salvage operations begin. The capsized vessel, left, is the battleship* Oklahoma.

ment going to war. The chances of this occurring seemed fairly remote, however, and Yamamoto took the opportunity to draft his final orders. On 6 November a full-scale dress rehearsal of the attack took place, involving all six carriers, and 350 aircraft staged a successful mock attack on a target 200 miles from the launching zone. Twenty-four hours later Nagumo was informed that Y-day – the day of attack – would be Sunday, 7 December (Hawaii time) and ordered to assemble his fleet at Tankan Bay on Etorofu, the largest of the Kurile Islands, by 22 November. The ships began to leave their bases on 17 November; 27 submarines, known as the Advanced Expeditionary Force, set out for Hawaii between 18 and 20 November. By 22 November all six carriers, together with two battleships, two heavy cruisers, one light cruiser, nine destroyers and eight fleet tankers, were ready to go. They set sail before dawn on 26 November, following a northerly route in over-cast and stormy conditions, hoping to avoid detection for the whole of their 12-day voyage.

In retrospect, the maintenance of secrecy is surprising, for since August 1940 the Americans had been able to read all Japanese diplomatic communications, having cracked the relevant code. But there was never any direct mention of Operation Z, and so long as negotiations continued in Washington, the possibility of a sudden Japanese attack seemed remote. Even if this had not been the case, there was no reason to suppose that Pearl Harbor would be the primary target. It was a long way from Japan, necessitating the formation of a naval force which did not appear to exist (US Intelligence, fooled by false radio traffic, reported all Japanese carriers to be 'still in home waters' as late as 27 November), and seemed contrary to known Japanese aspirations toward the Dutch East Indies. An aura of complacency gradually emerged, to be reflected tragically in a total lack of defensive preparations in Hawaii. By the weekend of 6/7 December the fleet was still following peacetime routines, aerial reconnaissance was restricted to sea areas to the south and west, torpedo nets across the mouth of the harbor were rarely kept in place, and security was lax. Even when one of the Japanese midget submarines was spotted and sunk by the USS *Condor* at 0635 hours on 7 December, no one in authority showed any interest.

The midget submarine was, in fact, one of three which approached the American base, acting upon orders received by the entire Japanese force on 2 December, after the Emperor had finally decided that war was unavoidable. The other two entered Pearl Harbor before dawn on 7 December, taking advantage of American neglect to close the torpedo nets across the harbor mouth between 0600 hours and 0840 hours. Meanwhile, Nagumo's force had reached the launching zone, 230 miles due north of Oahu, and the decision to go ahead had been made, despite reports that the American carriers were absent from their usual anchorages. In fact, *Saratoga* was undergoing repairs on the west coast of the United States, the *Lexington* was ferrying aircraft to Midway, and the *Enterprise* was returning to Pearl Harbor from Wake Island. But with a reported nine battleships, seven cruisers, three submarine-tenders and 20 destroyers at anchor, with no visible defensive screen, the opportunity seemed too good to miss. In the event, the count was not exact – only eight battleships were present and some of the other vessels had been wrongly described – but the discrepancies were minor. Fortunately for the Americans, the absence of carriers was to prove the difference between short-term disaster and long-term defeat.

Fuchida roared off the deck of the *Akagi* at precisely 0600 hours on 7 December, and within 15 minutes the first wave of the attacking force, comprising 43 fighters, 49 high-level bombers, 51 dive bombers and 40 torpedo bombers, had been successfully launched. Following a direct route at approximately 200 mph, the aircraft crossed the Oahu shoreline at 0740 hours to achieve complete surprise. Visibility was excellent, enabling the Japanese airmen to see American fighters and bombers lined up in neat rows in front of their hangars and the fleet at anchor, apparently deserted. Fuchida transmitted the radio message 'Tora, Tora, Tora' – a prearranged code to signify to his superiors in Japan that surprise had been achieved and all was well – and signaled his pilots to follow the first of their practiced plans, whereby the torpedo bombers would go in first, followed by the high-level bombers, leaving the dive bombers and fighters to bring up the rear. As it happened, in the confusion and excitement of the attack, such order rapidly disappeared, but this merely served to add to the surprise and chaos on the ground. At 0755 hours, the first bombs began to fall.

From the beginning of Yamamoto's planning, the fear of a positive American reaction in the air had been uppermost in Japanese minds, particularly when it was estimated that 455 aircraft

ABOVE: *A wrecked P40 fighter on Wheeler Field, also heavily hit on December 7th.*

ABOVE RIGHT: *Close up of the damage to the destroyer* Downes *in the dry dock at Pearl Harbor.*

RIGHT: *Repair operations to the old cruiser* Raleigh *after the Japanese attack.*

OVERLEAF, p34-35: *Attempts are made to rescue men trapped inside the hull of the capsized* Oklahoma.

would be stationed on Oahu at the time of the attack, and for this reason the initial assault was put in against the various Hawaiian airfields. Val dive bombers, with Zero fighter support, concentrated upon Hickam Field and Ford Island, as well as the Wheeler air base. At the latter, American fighters were lined up as if awaiting inspection, and in the first few minutes 20 P-40s and P-36s were destroyed. At Hickam, some 70 bombers – of which 12 were newly-delivered B-17s – were burned out, and similar pictures emerged at Kaneohe, a flying-boat base, and Ewa, an uncompleted Marine Corps airfield. Within a very short time, American air defense potential had been virtually wiped out – there being, in fact, only 231 aircraft in the Hawaii region – and the Japanese had gained complete air supremacy, enabling the other portions of Fuchida's force to attack the fleet with relative impunity.

The assault upon the battleships began shortly after 0800 hours, with Kate torpedo bombers, divided into two groups, making three successive low, fast runs against minimal opposition. An enormous amount of damage was done. In the first attack the battleships *California*, *Oklahoma* and *West Virginia* were hit; in the second the cruiser *Helena* was struck and the minelayer *Oglala* capsized; in the third the cruiser *Raleigh* and the aged battleship *Utah*, recently used by the Americans as a target ship, were torpedoed. At the same time the dive bombers plummeted down, making eight separate attacks from different points of the compass. Their aim was good – a product of the intense training at Kagoshima Bay – and the results were catastrophic. The battleships *Nevada*, *Maryland*, *Pennsylvania* and *Tennessee* all caught fire, while the *Arizona*, hit in the forward magazine and boilers, blew up and capsized, showering huge fragments of debris over the harbor. Four hundred seamen were trapped in her upturned hull. Permitting no respite, Fuchida himself led the high-level bombers into the attack, organizing all 49 into a single column and passing over the harbor at 12,000 ft. By now the Americans had recovered sufficiently to put up anti-aircraft fire, and as Fuchida's force wheeled round for a second run, two bombers were shot down and a third forced to ram its target. Unperturbed, the bombers made a third and final run, pouring their armor-piercing bombs onto the burning ships, before climbing to 15,000 ft and making way for the second wave. It was 0840 hours.

By this time all seven front-line battleships were on fire, and when the second wave of 170 aircraft arrived, led by Lieutenant Commander Shimazaki Shigekazu of the *Zuikaku*, their task was not made easy by billowing clouds of smoke. Nevertheless, a force of 80 Val dive bombers, briefed to hit the absent American carriers, mounted a furious assault upon the battleships, concentrating upon those which were still capable of putting up anti-aircraft fire. The *Nevada* tried to escape by slipping anchor and making for the harbor mouth, but was pounced on and torpedoed. Wallowing dangerously and threatening to sink in the middle of the channel, blocking it to all traffic, she had to be nursed to the shore and beached. Meanwhile the high-level bombers of the second wave had revisited the air bases, destroying surviving aircraft and installations at Hickam, Wheeler, Ford Island and Kaneohe. At the latter they were joined by 31 Zero fighters, whose original task of acting as a protective air umbrella had proved unnecessary. At 0945 hours, after nearly two hours sustained assault, the Japanese withdrew.

Fuchida's first wave aircraft reached their carriers at 1000 hours, to be followed two hours later by the last of Shimazaki's force, and when it was found that only 29 machines had been lost out of the 353 committed, the pilots were understandably ecstatic, demanding permission to

mount another attack. This would have been quite feasible, but Nagumo, worried that the missing American carriers were even then steaming to intercept him, refused. The task force turned for home, transmitting Fuchida's report – 'Four battleships definitely sunk, and considerable damage inflicted on the airfields.' It looked like a crippling blow.

Few people on Oahu at the time would have argued against this assessment. By noon on 7 December eight battleships, three cruisers, three destroyers and eight auxiliary craft – totaling some 300,000 tons – had been immobilized; Hickam, Wheeler, Ford Island and Kaneohe had been destroyed, together with 96 of the 231 aircraft in Hawaii (in fact only seven of the remaining machines were immediately airworthy); and over 3400 people had been killed or wounded. The only success had been against the midget submarines, all of which had been sunk before they could inflict any damage, but this was minor compared to the sheer shock and force of the Japanese assault. In what looked like a treacherous pre-emptive strike – because of translation problems the actual Japanese severance of negotiations was not delivered to President Roosevelt until after the attack had finished – the US Pacific Fleet had been virtually wiped out, enabling the enemy to advance into the Southwest Pacific, free from interference.

But the Japanese victory was in fact far from complete. The fatal flaw was that the strike had missed the US carriers entirely, so sparing a weapon which was to have decisive effects upon the future conduct of the war. American admirals, denied their traditional dependence upon the battleship, were forced to tear up existing plans and, of necessity, concentrate their attentions upon the role of naval air power. Because the *Saratoga*, *Enterprise* and *Lexington* escaped Pearl Harbor, the carrier had to replace the battleship as the central feature of fleet organization, rapidly becoming the principal naval weapon. The Americans were quick to learn, using their carriers successfully at the Battles of the Coral Sea, Midway, Philippine Sea and Leyte Gulf to beat the Japanese at their own game. In addition, Fuchida's airmen had failed to destroy the oil tanks, machine shops and other installations on Oahu and, despite the depressing picture on 7 December, Pearl Harbor itself was quick to recover from the blow. Of the eight battleships attacked, all but two were later raised and repaired, as were many of the smaller ships, and in the end the catalog of total destruction contained the names of the *Arizona*, *Oklahoma* and two destroyers only.

2.
Japan's Days of Triumph

Japan's attack on Pearl Harbor was but one part of her offensive to neutralize European forces in East and Southeast Asia and create by force the Greater East Asia Co-Prosperity Sphere Japanese leaders had talked about only a year before. Even as the Japanese task force steamed toward Hawaii, Japanese forces were poised and ready to occupy Burma, Hong Kong, Malaya, and the Philippines.

When news of the attack on Pearl Harbor reached the American command in Manila, a Japanese strike force was already off the Philippine coast. Although General Douglas MacArthur and Admiral Thomas Hart had been forewarned of the imminence of a Japanese attack by the War Department as early as 27 November 1941, defensive preparations were still incomplete when the Japanese struck at

ABOVE: *Nakajima Nell bombers on a mission over the Philippines during the early Japanese advances.*

LEFT: *General Sugiyama, Chief of Staff of the Japanese Army at the time of the Philippines' invasion.*

0530 on the morning of 8 December (Philippines time). From air bases on Formosa, the Japanese attacked American installations throughout the Philippine archipelago, literally destroying Clark, Nichols, and Iba air stations and neutralizing the United States Army Air Force just as effectively as the Pacific Fleet had been destroyed only hours before. The Asiatic Fleet, stationed in Manila Bay, was also badly mauled, leaving the American government virtually powerless to prevent Japanese forces from overrunning the islands despite the heroic defense put up by American forces and Filipino scouts.

Japanese forces were landed on Luzon on 10 December and in the weeks that followed, similar landings were made elsewhere on the island. Since American forces were powerless to prevent or hamper these amphibious operations, plans were hastily drawn up for a withdrawal of American and Filipino forces to Corregidor and the Bataan Peninsula. MacArthur and Hart hoped that such a strategic withdrawal would buy time until reinforcements were sent. Unfortunately for them, this proved impossible

given Japan's almost complete control over the air and shipping lanes around the Philippines.

Although American and Filipino forces fought valiantly to preserve their positions, resistance proved hopeless. On 11 March 1942 MacArthur was ordered to leave for Australia, leaving command of the garrison on the Bataan Peninsula to General Jonathan Wainwright. Wainwright and his men were able to hold on until 8 April when they evacuated the peninsula to the 'safety' of the Corregidor fortress. There, the American and Filipino survivors held out until 6 May when the garrison surrendered to the Japanese. This was the worst US defeat in the war to that date and marked the temporary end of American colonial rule in the Philippines. General MacArthur might vow to avenge this defeat and 'return' to the Islands, but as of June 1942, the Philippines had been added to the Japanese Empire.

The Japanese attack on the Philippines was mirrored by a similar attack on British Malaya which was launched on the same morning as the first Japanese air raids against Clark, Nichols and Iba fields. Unlike the Americans, who had

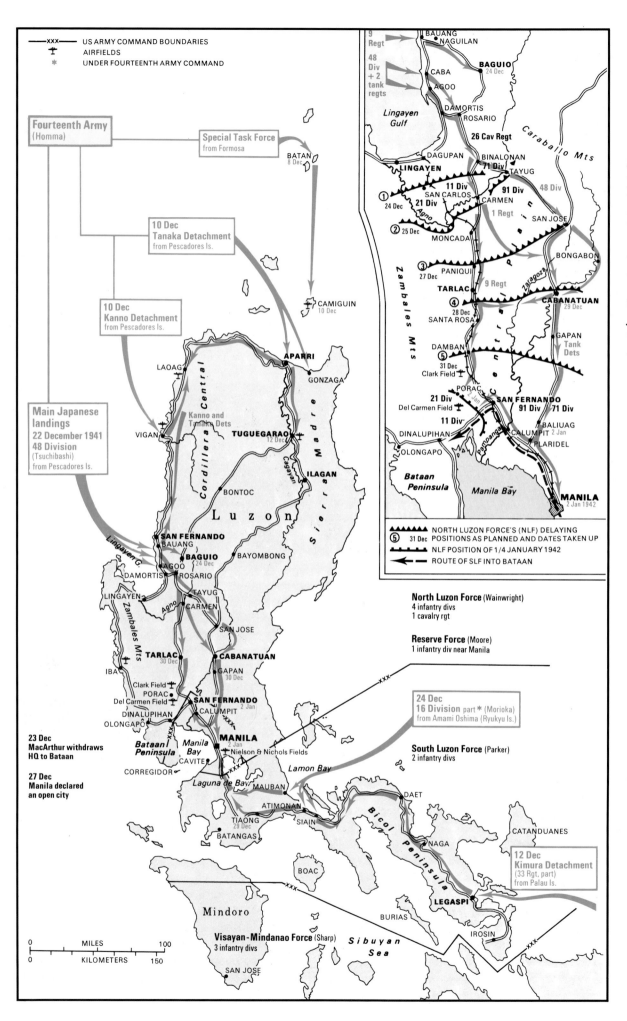

Fourteenth Army (Homma)

KEY

━━━ xxx ━━━	US ARMY COMMAND BOUNDARIES
⟂	AIRFIELDS
✳	UNDER FOURTEENTH ARMY COMMAND

Fourteenth Army (Homma)

Special Task Force from Formosa
BATAN 8 Dec

10 Dec Tanaka Detachment from Pescadores Is.

10 Dec Kanno Detachment from Pescadores Is.

⟂ CAMIGUIN 10 Dec

Main Japanese landings 22 December 1941 48 Division (Tsuchibashi) from Pescadores Is.

LAOAG
APARRI
GONZAGA
VIGAN ⟂
Kanno and Tanaka Dets
TUGUEGARAO 12 Dec
BONTOC
ILAGAN
Cordillera Central
Cagayan
Sierra Madre
Luzon
SAN FERNANDO
BAUANG
BAGUIO 24 Dec
BAYOMBONG
AGOO
DAMORTIS
ROSARIO
LINGAYEN
Lingayen G.
Agno
TAYUG
CARMEN
SAN JOSE
Zambales Mts
TARLAC 30 Dec
CABANATUAN
IBA ⟂
GAPAN 30 Dec
Clark Field ⟂
PORAC
Del Carmen Field ⟂
SAN FERNANDO 2 Jan
DINALUPIHAN
CALUMPIT
OLONGAPO
MANILA 2 Jan
Bataan Peninsula
Manila Bay
Nielson & Nichols Fields
CAVITE
CORREGIDOR
Laguna de Bay
MAUBAN
Lamon Bay
ATIMONAN
TIAONG 29 Dec
SIAIN
BATANGAS
Bicol Peninsula
DAET
NAGA
CATANDUANES
BOAC
Mindoro
SAN JOSE
BURIAS
Sibuyan Sea
IROSIN
LEGASPI

12 Dec Kimura Detachment (33 Rgt, part) from Palau Is.

23 Dec MacArthur withdraws HQ to Bataan

27 Dec Manila declared an open city

North Luzon Force (Wainwright) 4 infantry divs 1 cavalry rgt

Reserve Force (Moore) 1 infantry div near Manila

24 Dec 16 Division part ✳ (Morioka) from Amami Oshima (Ryukyu Is.)

South Luzon Force (Parker) 2 infantry divs

Visayan-Mindanao Force (Sharp) 3 infantry divs

SCALE:
0 — MILES — 100
0 — KILOMETERS — 150

(Inset map — northern Luzon)

9 Regt
BAUANG
NAGUILAN
48 Div +2 tank regts
BAGUIO 24 Dec
CABA
AGOO
Lingayen Gulf
DAMORTIS
ROSARIO
26 Cav Regt
Caraballo Mts
DAGUPAN
BINALONAN
LINGAYEN
71 Div
TAYUG
① 24 Dec
11 Div
SAN CARLOS
91 Div
48 Div
21 Div
CARMEN
② 25 Dec
Agno
MONCADA
1 Regt
SAN JOSE
③ 27 Dec
PANIQUI
BONGABON
Zambales Mts
TARLAC
9 Regt
Tarlac
④ 28 Dec
SANTA ROSA
CABANATUAN 29 Dec
GAPAN Tank Dets
DAMBAN
⑤ 31 Dec
Clark Field
PORAC 2 Jan
21 Div
Del Carmen Field
SAN FERNANDO
91 Div
71 Div
11 Div
BALIUAG
CALUMPIT 2 Jan
DINALUPIHAN
Pampanga
PLARIDEL
OLONGAPO
Bataan Peninsula
Manila Bay
MANILA 2 Jan 1942

Inset key:

▲▲▲▲	NORTH LUZON FORCE'S (NLF) DELAYING
⑤ 31 Dec	POSITIONS AS PLANNED AND DATES TAKEN UP
━▲━	NLF POSITION OF 1/4 JANUARY 1942
◄━ ━	ROUTE OF SLF INTO BATAAN

LEFT: *The early stages of the Japanese conquest of Luzon and the planned American and Filipino retreat to the Bataan Peninsula.*

RIGHT: *A large proportion of the force defending the Philippines was locally recruited like these Filipino Scouts. Their training and equipment were poor, however.*

BELOW RIGHT: *Japanese troops land in Lingayen Gulf, 22 December 1941.*

little advance warning of the attack on Pearl Harbor and the Philippines, the British command in Malaya and Singapore had been aware of the imminence of the Japanese attack for weeks but had taken few measures to prepare for such an attack except to put the fleet at Singapore on full alert. The reason for this seemingly casual attitude reflected the confidence of the Royal Navy and Air Force that British naval and aerial forces were sufficiently strong to repel a Japanese offensive.

Ordered not to violate the Thai border, Air Marshal Sir Robert Brooke-Popham, commander of British forces in Malaya, had to wait for the Japanese to move first, assuming that their advance could be blunted by deploying British forces in a line across the Kra Isthmus. He reasoned that such a defensive deployment would buy sufficient time for the British to rush reinforcements to the area, thus allowing them to cross the border and take the ports of Singora and Patani in Siam. Failing in this, the British expected to be able to cut the railway line between Singora and the town of Jitra in Malaya, slowing the Japanese advance in the process and providing time for additional mobilization and deployment of forces in Malaya.

The failure of the British to make a pre-emptive strike across the Thai border was to cost dearly, for when the Japanese did cross the frontier on 8 December 1941 their numbers were such that the British had neither time nor sufficient manpower to strike toward Singora and Patani nor could they keep the Japanese from breaching their line across the Kra Isthmus. Within four days after they crossed the Malay border, Japanese forces had broken the British line, forcing the hasty evacuation of British forces to the south.

As British forces tried to prevent the southward movement of Japanese troops into Malaya, the British Navy suffered a significant setback when two capital ships, the *Prince of Wales* and the *Repulse*, were destroyed off the Malayan coast on 10 December. The loss of these two battlewagons ultimately crippled the defense of Singapore and Malaya. Thanks to the absence of effective naval resistance, the Japanese had no trouble landing troops along the Malayan coast, sealing the fate of the British in the process.

Within a month after launching their attack into Malaya, Japanese forces had reached Johore and were preparing to attack Singapore. By this time the seriousness of the Japanese threat was clear to all and the new commander of British forces in Malaya, General Sir Archibald Wavell ordered his forces to hold Johore at all costs until such time as reinforcements might be sent north and a counterattack launched. As Wavell understood, if Johore fell, then Singapore could not be defended. If Singapore fell, then the Dutch East Indies would be threatened. Thus, the defense of Malaya was not only important to the British.

In order to defend Johore, British forces north of Kuala Lumpur had to be diverted to the south. In so doing, however, the British surrendered control of much of their colony to the Japanese who were now free to move troops southward without fear of molestation. Because the Japanese were prepared for a rapid thrust south whereas the British were not, they were able to move their forces into Johore before British reinforcements from the Kuala Lumpur area arrived. The result was that British forces were overrun. By the end of the first week in February 1942, Johore was in Japanese hands and Japanese forces were ready to attack Singapore itself.

The Japanese attack on Singapore was launched on 8 February 1942, at which time two divisions crossed the straits from the mainland into Singapore. By the next day almost 15,000 Japanese troops had successfully penetrated Singapore, forcing the British to fall back to a

defensive posture. Unfortunately for them, once the straits were crossed Singapore did not offer a natural barrier similar to that of Corregidor or the Bataan Peninsula. Thus, defense of the colony proved hopeless. Furthermore, since the Japanese attacked the British naval station in Singapore from the north instead of by sea, the British could not defend even this enclave.

Singapore fell to the Japanese on 15 February 1942. Even more than the retreat of the Americans from the Philippines, the fall of Malaya and Singapore was a psychological defeat for the Allies of great importance. Conversely, for the Japanese this victory was sweet. Having neutralized the United States in Hawaii and the Philippines, they easily overran Malaya and Singapore whose British defenders had underestimated Japan's strength.

ABOVE: *The US flag is lowered on Corregidor island in Manila Bay, the last stronghold to be captured by the Japanese in the Philippines, 6 May 1942.*

RIGHT: *The British battleship* Prince of Wales *in Singapore just days before the outbreak of war.*

BELOW: *Crewmembers escape to an escorting destroyer from the sinking* Prince of Wales.

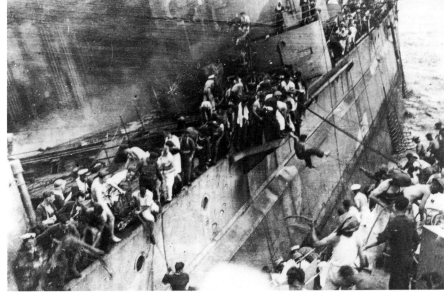

ABOVE RIGHT: *Admiral Tom Phillips (right) and his Chief of Staff, Admiral Paliser, on their arrival in Singapore. Phillips commanded the* Prince of Wales *and* Repulse. *It was unfortunate that Phillips was in this position because he was very traditional in his views regarding the role of battleships as the principal naval weapon.*

Even as the battle raged in the Philippines and Malaya, Japanese forces seized the Crown Colony of Hong Kong. The first Japanese troops entered the colony on 8 December 1941. By the end of the month, the British had surrendered. The relative ease with which the Japanese took Hong Kong reflected the isolation of the British garrison from command headquarters in Malaya. Whereas the Japanese had only to launch their offensive by moving troops across the Kwangtung border into Hong Kong and could bomb British installations from bases on Formosa, only 400 miles away, the nearest British reinforcements were in Malaya, almost 1500 miles away. Hong Kong clearly could not be defended yet the garrison was wastefully large

with substantial Canadian reinforcements rushed there late in the day to bolster the colony's defenses. Indeed, the Japanese not only succeeded in taking the colony in less than a month; they captured over 12,000 of the British-Canadian defense forces, almost the entire reinforced garrison in the colony of Hong Kong.

With Malaya in their hands, the Japanese initiated an invasion of the Dutch East Indies. After their victory in the Battle of the Java Sea, 27-28 February 1942, Japanese forces landed on Java. Nine days later, the Dutch colonial regime capitulated. For the Japanese, the occupation of the Indies was the culmination of years of effort to gain access to and control over the oil fields and refineries in the Dutch colony. As an industrial power almost totally dependent upon petroleum imports, Japan had covetously eyed the Indies for over a decade. Fearing, however, that any precipitate action against the Dutch might inflame American opinion, the Japanese carefully avoided use or threat of force against the Dutch, preferring to try diplomacy. Thus, in 1940 and again in 1941, the Japanese tried to persuade the Dutch to raise the amount of petroleum products exported to Japan and to permit Japanese interests to explore and develop new oil fields in the Indies. Such suggestions fell on deaf ears, although some concessions of a minor nature were granted.

Although the Dutch were in no position to withstand a Japanese attack, they doggedly refused to knuckle under to diplomatic efforts to give Japan control over the petroleum industry in the Indies. Frustrated in two successive efforts to 'open up' the Indies, the Japanese laid plans for a more direct effort to incorporate the colony into the Greater East Asia Co-Prosperity Sphere. As early as October 1940, the Imperial Army and Navy were instructed to draw up contingency plans for an occupation of the islands. Furthermore, Japanese intelligence operatives were instructed to step up their program of assistance to Indonesian nationalist groups so that in the event of an armed attack, the Dutch would find themselves facing internal and external enemies.

Japanese-Dutch talks relative to the Indies came to an end in June 1941 when the Tokyo government withdrew its negotiators from Batavia after failing to secure meaningful concessions

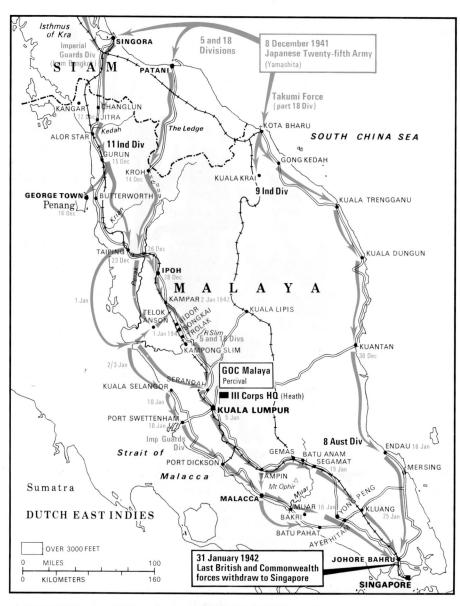

ABOVE: *The Japanese conquest of Malaya.*

LEFT: *Japanese troops land on Hong Kong island. Before the war it had been recognized that Hong Kong was impossible to defend against the large Japanese forces that could be assembled over the border in China. However, the garrison was wastefully increased shortly before the outbreak by a force including a large number of Canadian troops.*

from the Dutch. Contingency plans for an invasion of the Indies were now to be effected and coordinated with the overall grand strategy which had been approved at an Imperial Conference on 6 September 1941. Where diplomacy had failed, war would triumph.

The Japanese attack force which invaded the Indies in 1942 enjoyed an advantage not shared by similar task forces in Malaya and the Philippines, namely the support of the nationalist movements in the islands. In Indonesia the Japanese came not as conquerors but, rather, as liberators. Pro-Japanese sympathy, which had been strong even before the invasion, increased as the invaders made headway against the Dutch. Such support had been carefully cultivated before the war when Japanese operatives infiltrated Muslim and secular nationalist groups and it was enhanced by the relative ease with which the Japanese despatched Dutch forces. The psychological impact of Japan's humiliation of the Dutch was tremendous, dissipating what support existed for the Dutch from Indonesian leaders.

The Dutch authorities, for their part, did little to exploit what anti-Japanese sentiment existed in the Indies, even as the Japanese invasion was in progress. Unfortunately for them, colonial

administrators had come to accept the propaganda emanating from the regime as reality, fully expecting the Indonesian masses to rally to their banner. To the contrary, the masses responded to the Japanese attack not with support of the Dutch but, rather, with violent attacks of their own against government and business leaders. Indeed, the Japanese had eventually to use considerable power of persuasion to restore order in Batavia and other urban centers. But now the Indies were under Japanese control, marking the culmination of a long cherished dream to bring this oil rich area into the Greater East Asia Co-Prosperity Sphere. After centuries of Dutch rule, the colonial system was suddenly destroyed. Although Indonesian nationalist leaders would soon find the Japanese more oppressive in their own way than the Dutch, for them the war and the Japanese occupation were to be an unprecedented opportunity, a milestone on the road to independence.

With Japanese forces attacking and occupying the Dutch East Indies, Hong Kong, Malaya, and the Philippines, it was only a matter of time before they launched an invasion of Burma, the last stop in their game plan calling for the creation of the Greater East Asia Co-Prosperity Sphere. In some respects, Burma was of special importance to the Japanese, since it was through the port of Rangoon and over the Burma Road that supplies were sent to the government of Generalissimo Chiang Kai-shek, permitting that government to continue to resist Japanese entreaties for the negotiation of a diplomatic settlement of the China Incident. With almost one million men tied down in the occupation force in China, the Japanese would continue to be hamstrung in the conduct of the war in the Pacific. Hence, the occupation of Burma and the subsequent closing of the Burma Road was a matter of considerable priority.

The Japanese launched their first attack against Burma on 23 December 1941. Unlike Japanese strikes against Malaya, the Philippines, and the Indies, the Japanese attack in Burma was initially limited to a series of air raids aimed at destroying warehouses and storage depots in Rangoon and other stops along the road into China. The results of these raids were devastating. Many of the dock facilities and warehouses were destroyed, and thousands of Burmese and Indian laborers were killed and/or injured. By January 1942 the city of Rangoon had been brought to a halt and thousands fled the city for the safety of the countryside. Fearing riots and pillaging British authorities were forced to impose martial law in Rangoon.

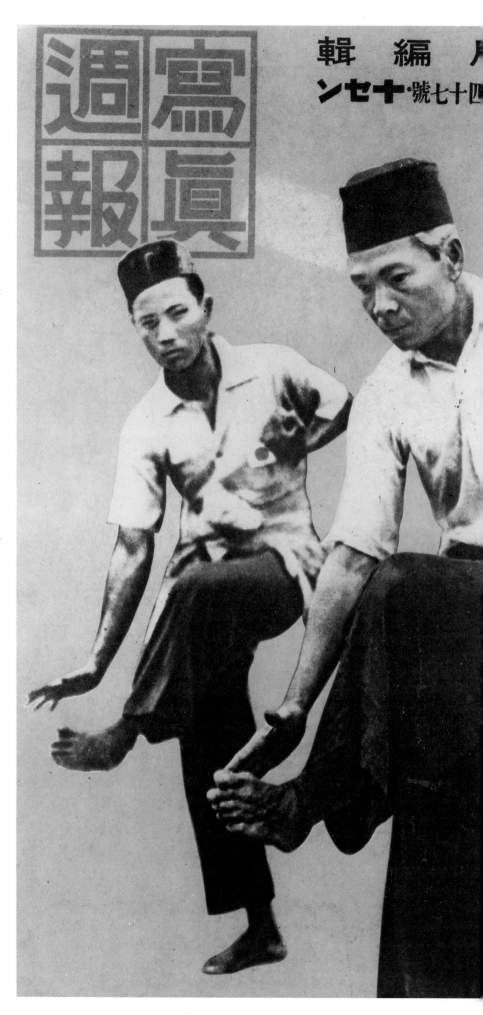

報 情
第・日八十月一十
昭和十三年二月十二日 第三種郵便物認可 昭和十七年十一月十八日發行（毎週一回水曜日發行） 第二百四十七號

LEFT: *A Japanese magazine depicts Indonesian nationalists celebrating their liberation from colonial rule.*

ABOVE: *Japanese tanks on the advance in Burma. Although the Japanese had few tanks they played an important part in their early victories.*

Japanese air raids against Rangoon and other installations, including rail heads and depots, were continued for three weeks in January 1942. Then, after aerial reconnaissance revealed the extent of the damage done and the havoc wreaked, Japanese land forces were sent across the Thai border on 20 January. It was Japan's purpose to cut the rail link between Rangoon and Kunming in China and then proceed south toward Rangoon.

The British were poorly equipped and ill-prepared to meet the Japanese advance. Once again, their disdain for the ability of the Japanese and exaggerated self-confidence was to prove a disaster. Not only did British commanders under-estimate the fury and rapidity with which Japanese forces poured into and across Burma, they stubbornly refused to accept offers of assistance from the Chinese Nationalists, for whom the Burma Road was a vital lifeline, until it was too late. It was only after Japanese forces broke through British defenses in the vicinity of the Sittang Bridge that Chinese aid was accepted and by this time, it was impossible to move Chinese forces into a position in which they might help to defend Rangoon and the supply route into China.

Having successfully defeated British and Indian forces in the vicinity of the Sittang, Japanese forces moved quickly toward Rangoon where the British were making hasty efforts to prepare for the defense of the city. As the Japanese moved closer to the city limits, Lend-Lease supplies destined for China were moved out as quickly as possible or jettisoned lest they fall into Japanese hands. By early March, the Japanese were poised around the city and on the 8th, they captured Rangoon, taking countless supplies in the process. Despite their efforts to prevent the Japanese from capturing this cache of aid, the British could not destroy it before the Japanese took the city. Thus, the Japanese victory in Rangoon was doubly sweet. Not only had they closed the main port of entry for supplies destined for Free China, they had also captured intact weaponry and ammunition which would facilitate the rest of their offensive in Burma.

As the British evacuated Rangoon, Japanese forces regrouped in the city before heading north towards Prome and Toungoo. It was the hope of the British and their Chinese allies that they might prevent the Japanese from capturing the Yenangyaung oil fields which lay north of Prome.

Since these fields constituted China's only source of crude oil, it was imperative that the line be held. Furthermore, if the Allies were able to hold the Japanese south of these cites, it might be possible to build a new supply route into China from Assam to Burma, linking the Indian ports of Calcutta and Chittagong to Yunnan, thus replacing the route from Rangoon. If this new line could not be held, the Japanese would easily overrun the rest of the colony.

Shortly after the middle of March 1942, Japanese forces marched northward from Rangoon. As they moved, they were harassed by air raids conducted by the RAF and Claire Chennault's American Volunteer Group, the Flying Tigers. Responding to these aerial attacks, the Japanese launched a series of massive air raids of their own, aimed at knocking out Anglo-American installations at Magwe and elsewhere. By the end of March, they had succeeded in forcing the evacuation of these bases and the destruction of Allied air strength in Burma.

Without air cover, British and Chinese forces were easy targets for the Japanese who had secured information relative to their whereabouts from aerial reconnaissance missions and Burmese nationalists. On 30 March Japanese forces took the city of Toungoo and shortly thereafter Prome as well. With Prome and Toungoo secured, the Japanese pushed on towards Lashio, the southern terminus of the Burma Road, which they took by 29 April. With the capture of Lashio, the Burma Road was finally closed, isolating China from the outside world except for the aerial route 'over the hump.'

The defense of Lashio marked the final Allied effort to hold Burma. Following their defeat there, the remnants of the Sino-British defense in Burma was hastily withdrawn to China and India. Before leaving Burma, Allied forces destroyed what equipment and supplies they could not carry and bombed the bridges across the Salween River after their evacuation. By June of 1942 the Japanese were in full control of Burma. The fleshing out of the Greater East Asia Co-Prosperity Sphere had been completed.

As had been the case in Indonesia, the Japanese occupation of Burma was aided and abetted by the co-operation of Burmese nationalist leaders who had been cultivated by the Japanese for at least a decade before their forces entered the colony. The British, on the other hand, had done little to rally nationalist leaders to their banner. Had they promised some measure of greater autonomy or independence at a later date, the Burmese might have stood with them after the outbreak of World War II.

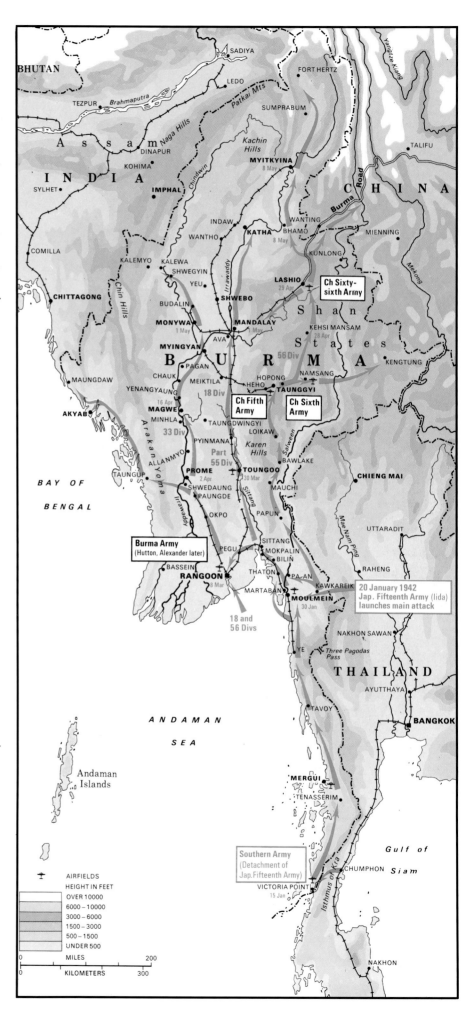

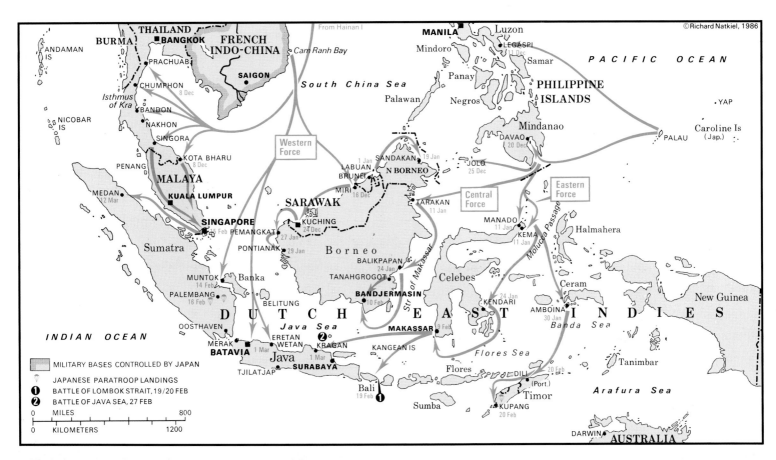

LEFT: *The Japanese conquest of Burma. As well as being British territory Burma was valued by the Allies as providing a route by which supplies could reach the Chinese Nationalists.*

TOP: *The overall Japanese plan for the conquest of the East Indies. Also noted are the naval battles of the Lombok Strait and the Java Sea in which the last Allied forces were defeated.*

ABOVE: *General Wavell (left) was appointed to a newly-created ABDA command at the end of 1941. Also shown are Admiral Hart and General Brett.*

Failing to do this, the British could hardly expect their 'wards' to flock to their banner when the war reached Burma. Not only did the Burmese not aid the British in their effort to defend the colony, they fought against them with groups like the Burmese Independence Army facilitating the Japanese conquest.

By May 1942 the Japanese had successfully completed their offensive and had they stuck to their original plan, they would have turned to a defensive strategy designed to consolidate and protect their new empire in East and Southeast Asia against an eventual Allied counterattack. In light of the ease and speed of their victories, however, Japanese leaders were reluctant to give up the momentum they had achieved following Pearl Harbor. In particular, the Imperial Navy was eager to finish the job they had started at Pearl Harbor where they had destroyed or incapacitated the battleships of the Pacific Fleet but missed the aircraft carriers which were at sea when the attack took place. As long as these ships remained, the United States would be in a position to menace Japanese forces and if they were augmented by the despatch of other vessels, the Pacific Fleet might once again constitute a serious challenge. Such a possibility dictated a second and decisive strike against the United States Navy.

In March 1942 the Imperial Navy proposed to expand Japan's perimeter in the Pacific by in-

itiating action to capture Port Moresby in New Guinea and Midway Island. It was hoped, at the same time, that what was left of the Pacific Fleet might be lured into battle near Midway and destroyed there. As envisaged by Japanese naval officers, the capture of Port Moresby would be a combined naval, aerial and land effort with Japanese forces assembling at Rabaul and off the island of Truk in the Carolines and proceeding toward the Coral Sea. This plan was presented and approved at an Imperial Conference in April 1942.

Easy successes had given the Japanese a contempt for the Americans. They had become infected, as the perceptive and intelligent Rear Admiral Hara Chuichi was to admit after the war, with 'victory disease.' It is always a mistake to underrate the enemy, and now the Japanese were falling into this error. Moreover, Japan's resources were simply inadequate for the manifold tasks her strategy imposed. The Japanese merchant navy had neither the tonnage nor the organization to supply her far-flung outposts. Nor had Japan the industrial capacity, or even

OVERLEAF: *Strike aircraft warm up on the deck of a US carrier during the Battle of the Coral Sea.*

the manpower, to build up a fleet sufficient to protect her long lines of communication. For sea power, as she herself proved, now meant carrier-borne air forces. And her early successes, due to superior pilots, planes and techniques, had not been won without loss. It is estimated that by April 1942 Japan had lost 855 naval planes, 315 in combat and 540 lost 'operationally.' These losses, were of course, replaced, but there was a decided fall in the quality of air crews. That Yamamoto was right to insist that the US Pacific Fleet must be destroyed by 1943 is certain. He knew very well that the United States with its tremendous economic and industrial capability could outbuild Japan.

In April 1942 the Japanese made a foray into the Indian Ocean, which effectively neutralized the small British forces in those waters. This done they turned their attention to Port Moresby, the first objective of the new strategy.

The Japanese believed that the Americans had only one carrier in the South Pacific. They thought up a complicated plan in which five forces, following different routes, but adhering to a set timetable would surprise the enemy and

engage them in an unequal fight. What they did not know was that American intelligence had actually broken their codes before the war, and could decipher many of their fleet messages. By 17 April the American Pacific Fleet had already unraveled the outline of the Japanese plan.

Vice-Admiral Inouye, commander of the Fourth Fleet, was the overall Japanese leader. His principal strike force was based around the carriers *Zuikaku* and *Shokaku* which were to pass down the eastern side of the Solomons before turning west to enter the Coral Sea. The initial move to set up a seaplane base at Tulagi in the southern Solomons was to be covered by a force based around the smaller but still powerful carrier *Shoho* and in addition a substantial transport force was to set out with the invasion units bound for Port Moresby. The Allied forces were led by Rear Admiral Frank Fletcher whose Task Force 17 had been rushed south to the area from Pearl Harbor. The principal component of this force was the carrier *Yorktown*. The *Lexington* was already present in the area with TF 11 and the Allied force was completed by an Australian and American cruiser squadron, TF 44.

RIGHT: *US naval forces carried out a number of Pacific operations in the early months of 1942 to recover some of the initiative lost at Pearl Harbor. One such was an attack on Japanese bases in the Marshall and Gilbert Islands on 1 February 1942. Guns aboard the heavy cruiser* Northampton *are shown shelling Wotje Atoll during this attack.*

The actual sequence of events is perhaps best understood in the form of a timetable:

1 May

Tulagi Invasion Group (Shima) set sail from Rabaul.

Task Forces 11 and 17 rendezvoused north of New Caledonia.

2 May

Reconnaissance plane sighted Shima's force, but the reports which reached Fletcher were not clear. So Fletcher moved northwest with Task Force 17.

Then the Japanese were sighted approaching Tulagi, from which island the small Australian garrison withdrew.

3 May

In the evening, one of MacArthur's scout planes reported Japanese landing on Tulagi. Fletcher in the *Yorktown* made for Tulagi.

4 May

A dawn strike on Tulagi by over 40 American planes sank one destroyer, three small mine-sweepers and destroyed five seaplanes. Inexperienced pilots gave glowing reports of this modest score. Fletcher moved south to rendezvous with Fitch's TF 11. Crace (TF 44) joined Fitch. Takagi's carriers were still out of range, far from Coral Sea.

5 May

Fletcher concentrated his task forces, and re-fueled from the tanker, *Neosho*. Reconnaissance reports produced a confused picture. Fletcher decided in the evening to set course northwest toward the probable route of the Port Moresby Invasion Force.

Takagi's Carrier Striking Force rounded San Cristobal and turned northwest into the Coral Sea. Neither Admiral had any real idea of the size and position of his opponent's fleet.

6 May

Awaiting intelligence Fletcher turned south-east while refueling. In the morning, Takagi set a southerly course, which he hoped would bring him into contact with Fletcher, but he did not send out any reconnaissance planes! A plane from Rabaul spotted Fletcher's force, but this report did not reach Takagi until the next day. American reconnaissance, due to low cloud, failed to locate Takagi, who was only 70 miles from Fletcher's task force.

7 May

Takagi launched an air search at dawn, when he and Fletcher were some 200 miles apart. At 0736 hours, a report reached Takagi of one carrier and one cruiser, 200 miles south-south-west. Takagi thought this was the *only* US carrier in the South Pacific, and launched a major strike:

36 Val dive bombers, 24 Kate torpedo bombers, 18 Zeros as cover. The target turned out to be the tanker *Neosho* and the destroyer *Sims*, which were duly sunk. Reconnaissance planes from one of Goto's cruisers reported the true position of the American carriers. Fletcher decided to detach Crace, who was to wait south of the Jomard Passage in order to block the route of the invasion convoy. The American carriers turned north and launched a major air search, but the Japanese fleet was still concealed by bad weather. At 0815 hours, planes from the *York-town* reported two heavy cruisers and two destroyers as two carriers and four heavy cruisers 175 miles northwest of the American force. Fletcher assumed, not unreasonably, that this was the main Japanese force and launched a major strike.

Thus, like Takagi, Fletcher had sent a major strike against a minor target, and was himself vulnerable to shore- or carrier-based attack. Another plane reported a Japanese carrier and other ships in the same target area, so Fletcher did *not* recall his strike. (This second force was Goto's covering group, protecting the Port Moresby Invasion Force.) At 1100 hours, attack groups from the *Lexington* sighted Goto and attacked the *Shoho* by dive bombing from 18,000 ft. The Japanese Combat Air Patrol shot down one Dauntless, and lost eight fighters. The *Shoho* was sunk in ten minutes, and the strike leader signaled: 'Scratch one flattop.'

At 1338 hours, the *Lexington*'s force returned from their mission having lost three planes. Admiral Inouye at his headquarters in Rabaul, informed of Crace's position, and of the loss of the *Shoho*, ordered Shima to hold the Port Moresby Invasion Force at a safe distance north of the Lousiades, so Goto followed Shima. In a mix-up over identification three of MacArthur's B-17s from Townsville, Queensland, attacked Crace, who managed to beat them off!

Then Task Force 44 came under attack from 31 Japanese shore-based bombers, but Crace handled his ships brilliantly, and not one was hit. The Japanese reported the destruction of two battleships and a heavy cruiser.

In the late afternoon Takagi sent out a search-mission: 12 Vals and 15 Kates. (No Zeros as they were not capable of night operations.) The search proving fruitless they jettisoned bombs and torpedoes and made for home. Their course took them over Fletcher's fleet, which got 20 minutes warning from radar. His Combat Air Patrol of Wildcats shot down eight Kates. Vals shot down two Wildcats, for the loss of one.

At dusk, three Japanese aircraft attempted to

land on the *Lexington* and three on the *Yorktown*, because they had lost their way. Only seven of the 27 Japanese planes landed safely back on their carriers.

Takagi, after considering an attempt to bring on a night action with his cruisers, decided that with the loss of the *Shoho* he must give the Invasion Force air protection. He turned north. Both admirals now had a good idea of the strength and position of their opponents. Each gave tactical command of his fleet to the most experienced carrier officer of flag rank. These were Aubrey Fitch and Hara Chuichi.

8 May
Hara decided to launch an early search 200 miles southeast and southwest. At dawn in heavy rain squalls Hara launched a strike force of 33 Vals, 18 Kates and 18 Zeros. It was airborne by the time the air search reported the American force 180 miles south, with its own air search launched.

A reconnaissance plane from the *Lexington* spotted the Japanese fleet soon after.

At 0915 hours, a strike force from the two US carriers made for the Japanese fleet, composed of 46 dive bombers, 21 torpedo bombers and 15 fighters. At 1057 hours 41 planes from the *Yorktown* attacked the *Shokaku*, while the *Zuikaku* was hidden in a rain squall. A Dauntless landed a 500 pound bomb on the *Shokaku* so that planes could no longer be launched from her flight deck.

The *Lexington*'s attack group was disorganized by the rain clouds, and many planes, unable to find the target, turned back. But four Dauntlesses and 11 Devastators went into the attack, scoring one bomb hit, killing 100 men, and starting a fire in the *Shokaku*. The strike cost the Americans 13 planes: five dive bombers, five torpedo bombers and three fighters.

Meanwhile the Japanese strike force, almost 70 planes, caught the American Combat Air Patrol low on fuel. Despite 20 minutes warning from radar, nine Wildcats did not have the altitude to meet the attack with advantage. The Japanese courageously pressed home their attack against unpracticed American antiaircraft gunners, in action for the first time. Surrounded by torpedo tracks the *Lexington*, unable to take avoiding action against them all, received two torpedo and two bomb hits. The *Yorktown*, with a smaller turning circle, received a bomb on her flight-deck, which, however, remained serviceable. By noon the battle was over.

The *Yorktown*, with 66 men killed by that single bomb was still in fighting trim, and her planes were still landing. The *Lexington*, listing seven degrees to port, was containing three

ABOVE: *The Japanese light carrier* Shoho *takes a torpedo hit during the Battle of the Coral Sea.*

RIGHT: *The USS* Lexington *is abandoned by her crew shortly before she was sunk. The US Navy greatly improved damage control procedures aboard carriers in the light of experience in the early Pacific battles.*

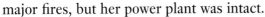

major fires, but her power plant was intact.

At 1247 hours, however, violent internal explosions shook the *Lexington*, resulting from gasoline fumes and finally threatened the ready bomb storage. The fires soon raged uncontrollably and at 1707 hours orders were given to abandon ship.

At 1853 hours using five torpedoes, a destroyer sank the *Lexington* with 35 planes still aboard her. Inouye, frightened at the prospect of intensive allied air activity, postponed the Port Moresby invasion, so the Allies had achieved their objective.

With the Port Moresby invasion foiled Admiral Nimitz ordered Fletcher to withdraw to protect the *Yorktown*.

Thus the battle ended. The Japanese had lost the *Shoho* while the Americans had lost the *Lexington*. The *Yorktown* had to go to Pearl Harbor for repairs, while the *Shokaku*, heavily damaged, had to limp back to Japan for repairs which took two months. The *Zuikaku* had so few planes left that she too had to go home for replacements. The Japanese had, however, lost 75 percent of their bomber pilots and planes.

So one could say that the Battle of the Coral Sea was a draw. But that is not really so. It was a battle that the Japanese might have been expected to win, but in which the Allies, with their inexperienced pilots, had held their own. Admirals Fletcher, Fitch and Crace had really deserved well of their countries!

The Americans emerged from the ordeal with clearer ideas on the tactical use of carriers. This was, of course, to serve them well at Midway and thereafter. More to the point, Coral Sea marked the high water mark of Japanese southward expansion. It was their first repulse. The level-headed and experienced Yamamoto found in it confirmation of his views that the further acquisition of territory, so far from helping Japan, would merely squander her exiguous resources.

Fortified by the prestige he had won at Pearl Harbor Yamamoto, quite correctly, now convinced his more conservative colleagues, that the paramount object of the Japanese Fleet must be to complete the destruction of the United States Pacific Fleet.

3.
Midway,
The Turning Point

idway Island is a flyspeck in the vast Pacific Ocean, about halfway between Pearl Harbor and Japan. It is, in fact, an atoll – two tiny islands almost entirely surrounded by a barrier reef. In the center of the atoll is a lagoon with a narrow ship channel leading to it, on the western edge an open harbor. A few insignificant bits of coral – but in June 1942, they were to become the object of one of the greatest naval battles of the war.

Admiral Yamamoto had presented his plans for the campaign to the General Staff at the beginning of April 1942. It called for luring the remnants of the American Pacific Fleet to the defense of the solitary outpost, forcing it into a decisive battle, and destroying it.

The Naval General Staff agreed that a decisive battle was necessary at that point in the war, but was not convinced that Midway, only 1136 miles west-northwest of Pearl Harbor, was the best place to fight it. Instead, many members advocated cutting the lines of communication between the US and Australia by advancing on the islands of Fiji and Samoa. In addition, Second Fleet objected on the grounds that it was not ready; Fourth Fleet, which was detailed to look after logistical problems following the occupation of the island, claimed it could not guarantee its ability to carry out this function even if the operation was successful; and First Air Fleet wanted to postpone the campaign to gain some time for rest and refitting after extensive operations in the Indian Ocean. Others pointed out that if the battle took place as planned, Japan's two most powerful carriers, the *Shokaku* and *Zuikaku*, would have to be left behind. But Yamamoto stood firm. One of Japan's greatest military geniuses, with the rare ability both to de-

BELOW LEFT: *A B-25 Mitchell bomber takes off from the carrier* Hornet *as the Doolittle Raid begins.*

BELOW: *Colonel Doolittle (front left) with Admiral Mitscher and some of Doolittle's men aboard the* Hornet *before the attack.*

vise original ideas and translate them into action, he had never been confident about his island country's ability to wage war against an industrial giant like the United States. Before the war he had warned the Premier, General Tojo Hideki, that 'if I am told to fight . . . I shall run wild for the first six months or a year, but I have utterly no confidence for the second and third years.' His outlook was not improved by the success of the Japanese attack on Pearl Harbor: he wrote to his sister. ' . . . in spite of all the clamor that is going on we could lose [the war]. I can only do my best.' He now felt that success at Midway was essential to Japan's survival. Eventually the General Staff gave in.

Just at this time, on 18 April, 16 B-25 bombers led by Lieutenant Colonel James Doolittle carried out a surprise attack on Tokyo from the aircraft carriers *Enterprise* and *Hornet*. They inflicted very little physical damage, but the psychological impact of this first attack on the Home Islands themselves was enormous. The Japanese had no idea where the raid came from (Roosevelt's comment that it had come from Shangri-La was not very helpful), and many suspected that it had originated from Midway. To the major goal of the Midway campaign – the destruction of the American fleet and subsequent mastery of the Pacific Ocean – was added another purpose: capture of the island would

protect the Emperor from the indignity of being bombed again. It would also mean the elimination of an important refueling base for US submarines and provide a base for future raids on Pearl Harbor.

On 5 May, then, Imperial General Headquarters issued the order: 'Commander in Chief Combined Fleet will, in co-operation with the Army, invade and occupy strategic points in the Western Aleutians and Midway Island.'

By that time the first phase in the great Japanese offensive – the campaign to achieve control of the Coral Sea by seizing Tulagi in the Solomon Islands and Port Moresby in Papua – was well underway. But the setback in the Battle of the Coral Sea – the first the Japanese had suffered – confirmed Yamamoto in his belief that top priority had to be given to the destruction of the rest of the American Fleet. Thus, the stage was set for the Midway campaign.

Yamamoto's battle plan was a complicated one, utilizing the diversionary tactics and division of forces that were always integral parts of Japanese strategy. The plan called for a strike on 3 June against Dutch Harbor in the Aleutians. Destruction of the American base and occupation of the western islands would not only secure

the northernmost anchors of Japan's proposed 'ribbon defense,' but would, he hoped, lure the US Pacific Fleet northward. While the Americans were rushing to defend the Aleutians the Japanese would bomb and occupy Midway by 5 June. Then when the American fleet returned Japanese planes based on the island and on carriers would mount an intensive bombing offensive. Any ships that escaped would be sunk by the Japanese battleships and cruisers.

Surprise was the key element in Yamamoto's plan; there was to be no challenge from the Americans until after Midway had been occupied. Even if the enemy did not take up the Aleutian challenge, they could not get to Midway before 7 June. And even if they did not contest the occupation, the pressure from Midway on Pearl Harbor would soon force them to counterattack.

The Japanese force was divided into five sections. An Advance Force of 16 submarines would harass the Americans as they approached Midway from either the Aleutians or Pearl Harbor. The Northern Area Force under Vice-Admiral Hosogaya consisted of the light carriers *Ryujo* and *Junyo*, along with two heavy cruisers, a destroyer screen, and four transport ships carrying

BELOW: *Out of fuel, a Dauntless ditches beside an American cruiser during the Battle of Midway. Navigating back to a parent carrier after combat was always difficult for aircraft crew.*

ABOVE: *A Dauntless prepares for take off from the* Yorktown *at Midway.*

troops for occupying the Aleutian islands of Adak, Attu, and Kiska.

The most power lay with Vice-Admiral Nagumo Chuichi's Main Striking Force: the four big carriers *Akagi, Kaga, Hiryu*, and *Soryu*, and their screen of destroyers and cruisers. Nagumo's task was to launch air strikes against Midway, to soften it up for Admiral Kondo Nobutake's Midway Occupation Force. Kondo had two battleships, six heavy cruisers, and many destroyers to support the 12 transports carrying a 5000-man occupation force.

Yamamoto was 300 miles behind Nagumo and Kondo, with the Main Body – a force composed of nine battleships and two light carriers, with their attendant cruiser and destroyer screen. He was flying his flag in the newly-constructed *Yamato* which, with its nine 18-inch guns, was the biggest and most powerful battleship in the world. There was little chance that the battleships, with a maximum gun range of only 40 miles, would play much part in the battle; some of Nagumo's younger officers claimed caustically that the battleship fleet was holding a naval review in the Pacific. But Yamamoto, despite the great importance that he gave to aircraft and carriers, still felt it necessary to compromise with the conservatives who still advocated big ships and big guns.

The Japanese Fleet contained almost the entire fighting force of the Japanese Navy – 162 ships including four heavy carriers, four light carriers, 11 battleships, 22 cruisers, 65 destroyers, and 21 submarines.

To counter the blow that Yamamoto was planning, the Americans had three carriers – the *Enterprise, Hornet*, and *Yorktown*, eight cruisers, and 15 destroyers. There were no battleships; they rested on the bottom of Pearl Harbor, except for a few stationed on the West Coast that were too old and too slow to be of any real use in modern warfare. But even that small force was more than Yamamoto had thought the Americans could assemble. He believed that the *Yorktown* had been sunk in the battle of the Coral Sea along with the *Lexington*, when in fact she had managed to limp back to Pearl Harbor. Much has been made of the fact that the carrier was repaired and reprovisioned in three days and three nights, when the job would normally have taken 90 days. But it would be far from accurate to imply that the repairs were anything other than rough jury-rigging. The hull was patched and damaged compartments were braced with timbers. But only a few of the watertight doors were fixed and three boilers that had been knocked out were not even touched. Maximum speed was reduced to 27 knots.

ABOVE: *The Japanese submarine* I-168 *which sank the already damaged* Yorktown *at Midway.*

The island of Midway itself served as a base for 54 Marine Corps planes (including 25 obsolete Brewster Buffalo fighters), 32 Navy Catalinas, and 23 Air Force planes (including 17 B-17s and six brand new Navy Avenger torpedo bombers). In addition to its planes, the island had two good search radars, was dotted with artillery, and had almost 3000 men in Army and Marine units dug in and protected by bombproof shelters throughout the island. The actual invasion never took place, but if it had there is no certainty it would have succeeded. Midway's defenses were as carefully prepared as Tarawa's would be later in the war, and Kondo's force of 5000 was not nearly as impressive as the American force that eventually took Tarawa.

Admiral Chester Nimitz, Commander in Chief of the Pacific Fleet, was the man charged with containing the Japanese threat. Nimitz was a 57-year-old Texan who had served in a variety of commands, including a stint in the submarine service during World War I. He had made Rear Admiral in 1938, had been promoted to admiral in 1941, and was given command of the Pacific Fleet following the raid on Pearl Harbor. His calm, confident manner and refusal to bring in new staff gradually rebuilt shattered morale, and even with the meager forces at his disposal he was able to organize raids on Japanese bases in the Marshall Islands, New Guinea, and New Britain during the spring of 1942.

Rear Admiral Fletcher, the spare, leathery veteran of the Coral Sea, was in tactical command of the forces mustered to defend Midway. Fletcher – 'Black Jack' Fletcher to his men, though his hair was blond and his eyes blue – was the commander of Task Force 17 built around the patched-up *Yorktown*. He had no control over the Midway-based forces, the submarines operating in the area, or the force sent to defend the Aleutians. Nor did he exercise much control over Task Force 16, which was centered on the *Enterprise* and the *Hornet*, under the temporary command of Rear Admiral Raymond Spruance; Rear Admiral William Halsey (mistakenly nicknamed 'Bull' by a confused journalist) was in hospital being treated for a skin disease.

With the vast area of the Central and South Pacific to defend and with only modest forces at his disposal, Nimitz would have found himself in difficulties many times had not the code-breaking service existed. By 10 May intelligence had already confirmed Nimitz's suspicions about the next Japanese objective – Midway. He even had the major details of Yamamoto's plan, along with his approximate schedule and routes. Nimitz was familiar enough with Yamamoto's philosophy and style to predict a full attack on the island, with the destruction of the American carriers as one of the primary objectives, even though some of his officers feared that it was all an elaborate deception designed to cover another attack on Pearl Harbor or the West Coast.

The North Pacific Task Force – two heavy cruisers, three light cruisers, a destroyer division, a nine-destroyer strike group, six S-Class submarines, and numerous other craft – was formed by 17 May and placed under the command of Rear Admiral Robert ('Fuzzy') Theobald. Theobald did not get to Kodiak, off the Alaskan coast, to take command until 27 May, however; and the main body of his fleet was still assembling when the Japanese attacked Dutch Harbor on 3 June.

Meanwhile, on 24 May, Fletcher received a high-priority, top secret message at Tongatabu in the Friendly Islands where he was refueling and repairing what damage he could after his pounding on the Coral Sea. 'What it said,' he later recalled, 'was simply this: Get the hell back here, quick.' Fletcher hoisted anchor almost immediately; 26 May marked the *Yorktown*'s hundredth day at sea without proper replenishment – a record unequaled by any other modern American warship up to that time – and on 27 May she was steaming up the channel to Pearl Harbor to the accompaniment of whistles, sirens, and cheers. On 28 May the *Hornet* and *Enterprise* left to take up their stations; *Yorktown* followed on 30 May. Fletcher and Spruance had received their orders: to ' . . . inflict maximum damage on the enemy by employing strong attrition attacks' (in other words, heavy air strikes). A further letter of instruction directed them to be 'governed by the principles of calculated risk.'

Nagumo's Japanese carrier force left their home base on 26 May, followed by Yamamoto and the Main Body on 28 May. Neither commander was feeling very happy; Yamamoto was suffering from stomach cramps caused by tension, and Nagumo was worried because his carriers and crews had had barely a month for maintenance and refresher training. He later commented, 'We participated in the battle with meager training and without knowledge of the enemy.' Morale among the men in the fleet was

ABOVE: *Admiral Nagumo was in direct command of the Japanese aircraft carrier force at the Battle of Midway.*

RIGHT: *The Japanese carrier* Hiryu *maneuvers safely away from American bombs during one of the early ineffective attacks on the Japanese fleet by Midway-based forces.*

OVERLEAF: *Running repairs are carried out aboard the* Yorktown.

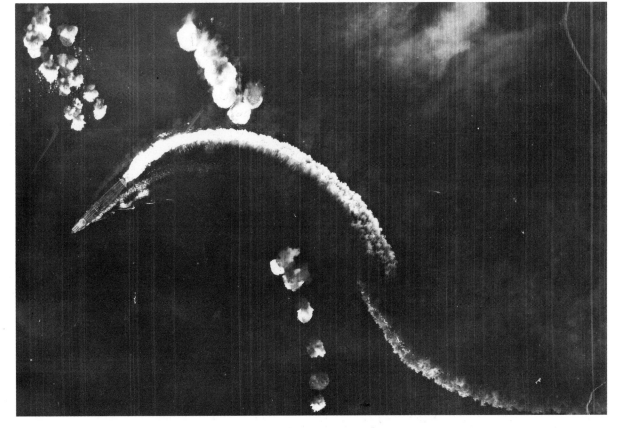

high, however. Meanwhile, Japanese submarines were taking up stations east of Midway to intercept any American ships sent out to relieve the island.

As they approached Midway from the west the Japanese Main Striking Force was shielded from patrolling American search planes by the many storms and fogs that occur in that area in May and June. Aboard his flagship, the carrier *Akagi*, Nagumo went over his plans for the last time. He decided to send 100 planes against Midway on 4 June and to hold back an equal number, including some torpedo planes, for a second wave. Of his many long-range scouts, which included cruiser and battleship float planes with a range of over 600 miles, seven would be detailed to keep a lookout for an enemy task force while Midway was being hit. They would cover an arc from due south to northeast; in the unlikely event that an American force should appear, the second wave could be sent against it.

Starting on 30 May, Nimitz began taking precautions to ensure against a Japanese sneak attack. The 22 Navy Catalina patrol bombers on Midway were sent on daily sweeps 700 miles out, and the Midway B-17s flew on daily search-attack missions to the area where the enemy was expected.

The waddling Catalinas were both the joy and despair of American pilots. They climbed, flew, and landed at almost the same slow speed and were armed only with .30 caliber machine guns in side blisters. The rumbling amphibians were death traps when corned by Japanese fighters, but their redeeming feature was that they could fly almost all day long without refueling.

Just before noon on 2 June Task Forces 16 and 17 – the *Yorktown* and her escorts, and the *Enterprise*, *Hornet* and their escorts – rendezvoused at 'Point Luck' about 325 miles northeast of Midway, and Fletcher took command.

The Battle of Midway opened at 0300 hours on 3 June, more than 1000 miles from the atoll itself, with the diversionary attack in the Aleutians. Theobald had deployed his force 400 miles south of Kodiak, fearing an attack on the American base at Dutch Harbor. Hosogaya's force slipped by the Americans easily in the fog and rain, however, and the base in the Eastern Aleutians was heavily bombed. The undefended islands of Attu and Kiska were occupied by the Japanese by 7 June, but the Army P-40s on Unmak convinced Hosogaya to bypass that island.

At 0843 hours the first sighting report was received from a Midway-based Catalina pilot, who continued to shadow the 11 Japanese ships he had found until 1100 hours. Fletcher concluded

rightly that they were not the large carrier force he was expecting; in fact, they were probably Kondo's Midway Occupation Force. Nine Army B-17s took off from Midway to attack the convoy, but made no hits. Fletcher, who was 300 miles east-northeast of Midway (and some 400 miles east of Nagumo), was certain that the Japanese carriers would approach the island from the northwest and strike the following day. Assuming that his presence was – and would remain – unknown, he hoped to be in a position to launch an attack against the carriers from their left flank as soon as the enemy planes had begun their strike against Midway. At 1931 hours on 3 June, he altered course to the southwest, which would bring him to a point some 200 miles north of Midway by morning. Through the night of 3-4 June the two carrier forces sailed toward each other on converging courses.

At 0430 hours on the morning of 4 June, 15 minutes after some 11 Catalinas had taken off from Midway to make another attempt to find the Japanese carriers, the *Yorktown* sent up ten dive bombers on a 100-mile search, as a routine precaution against the possibility of surprise. At the same time, 215 miles to the west, Nagumo was launching his first strike against Midway: 36 Nakajima B5N2 Kates, 36 Aichi D3A2 Vals, and 36 Mitsubichi A6M3 Zeros rose from the decks of their four carriers. By 0500 hours, the 108 Japanese planes were in formation, flying on a steady course for Midway.

Along with this first strike wave, Nagumo also sent up seven float planes to make a 300-mile reconnaissance. But no one in command really expected the American fleet to be anywhere near the area, and their overconfidence must have been transmitted to the search planes. Even though a seaplane from the heavy cruiser *Chikuma* passed almost directly over the US force and had an indecisive encounter with one of the *Yorktown*'s Dauntless dive bombers, it failed either to spot the American ships or to report the engagement, which would have been a sure sign of the presence of an American aircraft carrier in the vicinity.

At 0530 hours one of the Catalina pilots spotted the Japanese carriers through the heavy cloud cover and radioed a report back to Midway; the message was intercepted by the *Enterprise* and relayed to Fletcher on *Yorktown* at 0534 hours. A few minutes later, at 0545 hours, a second **PBY** radioed another message, without even bothering with code: 'Many planes headed Midway, repeat, Midway . . . .' The pilot then continued to shadow the Japanese ships, dodging the fighters that had been sent up to intercept him, until he was joined by other Catalinas who kept the carriers under constant surveillance from then on.

As soon as Fletcher had an approximate position for the Japanese force he signaled Spruance to proceed southwest with the *Enterprise* and *Hornet* and 'attack the enemy carriers when definitely located.' The *Yorktown* would wait to recover her search planes and obtain further information. At the same time (about 0530 hours) every plane on Midway was being ordered into the air in response to the Catalina's warning; by 0600 hours the only plane left on the ground was an old Grumman single-float biplane. Most of the interceptors were elderly, slow, Marine Corps Buffaloes – no match for the efficient new Zeros. But anti-aircraft fire on the island was good and about a third of the Japanese strike force was shot down. They had inflicted a fair amount of damage on the ground installations – barracks, mess halls, oil tanks, even the hospital. But casualties were light and the runways remained useable. Six new Navy Avenger torpedo bombers and four Army B-26s streaked after the recent attackers to counterattack, and 16 B-17s already in the air were also ordered to turn north and attack the Japanese carriers.

Nagumo's second strike force (93 planes) was waiting on the flight decks, armed with bombs and torpedoes, in case enemy surface forces appeared. But the returning planes from the first strike reported that the island would require another attack – a point that was emphasized by the appearance of the ten American planes from Midway even though they were not able to score a hit.

At 0715 hours Nagumo ordered the second wave planes taken below and rearmed with incendiary and fragmentation bombs for an attack on the island, clearing the decks for the return of the first wave; the entire process would take about an hour. Although in retrospect the order appears to have been a colossal blunder, at the time it seemed a reasonable move; Japanese scout planes had found no sign of an American surface force in the area, and Midway obviously had to be struck again since planes from the island had just attacked Nagumo's own ship.

But not quite 15 minutes later, at 0728 hours, the Admiral was amazed to receive the worst possible news from the *Chikuma*'s scout plane – a vague report that an 'estimated ten ships' had been sighted in the northeast. Nagumo paced the bridge for another 15 minutes, then asked the reconnaissance plane for more specific information. At 0809 hours the scout plane reported that the enemy force consisted of five cruisers and

five destroyers: at 0820 hours the pilot added that they were accompanied by 'what appears to be a carrier' (in fact was the *Yorktown*). Nagumo's worst fears had been realized, but he could not send his second wave off; the flight decks had to be kept clear to recover the first Midway strike force.

Following the first attack by the Avengers and B-26s the Japanese carrier force had been subjected to series of attacks, first by the Army B-17s, then by a flight of 11 old Vought SB2U Vindicators piloted by Marines, and finally by the submarine *Nautilus*, which had intercepted early reports of the Japanese position. Without fighter cover, however, all the planes were beaten off without scoring a single hit and the submarine was only able to fire one ineffective torpedo before she had to run for her life under a heavy Japanese depth charge attack. At this point Nagumo had been attacked by 52 American

ABOVE: *Damage to the* Yorktown's *superstructure following the second Japanese bomb hit.*

ABOVE: *A firefighting detail at work on board the* Yorktown.

planes and one submarine, and had not been touched; his fleet was intact while over half of the aircraft on Midway had been knocked out. As far as he knew he had only to launch one more strike at Midway and deal with one American carrier, but Spruance had already decided on a strategy and launched his own attack forces.

Spruance had originally intended waiting until 0900 hours when he would be about 100 miles from the enemy, but after discussions with his Chief of Staff, Captain Miles Browning, he decided to launch his planes early in hopes of catching the carriers while the Japanese attack planes were being rearmed and refueled. He sent up almost every operational plane he had – 67 Dauntless dive bombers, 29 torpedo bombers, and 20 Wildcats – holding back only 32 Wildcats for combat air patrol. The pilots were given orders based on the assumption that Nagumo would continue on his course toward

Midway until his strike planes were recovered at about 0900 hours.

Fletcher, in the *Yorktown*, had lost sight of Task Force 16 soon after he had sent it dashing on ahead; the two functioned almost as independent units through the rest of the battle. After he recovered his search planes he held back his own attack force for a time, waiting to see if any additional sighting reports would come in. When none did, he sent up his own planes at 0906 hours – 12 torpedo bombers, 17 dive bombers, and six Wildcats. Above his ship flew the Japanese scout plane, now joined by another float plane, from the cruiser *Tone*, beaming a homing signal to be used later to guide a strike force directly to the carrier.

Recovery operations had begun aboard the four Japanese carriers at 0837 hours, as they steamed toward Midway in a loose box formation – the *Hiryu* and *Kaga* to the east, *Soryu* and

Akagi to the west – inside a screen of two battleships, three cruisers, and 11 destroyers. But Nagumo was growing increasingly nervous as reconnaissance reports told him of a large force of carrier planes approaching; before his recovery was complete he turned east-northeast to contact the enemy carriers, while his crews worked hastily (and thus, somewhat carelessly) to rearm and refuel the planes.

Fortunately for the Japanese, this change in course caused 35 dive bombers and ten fighters from the *Hornet* to miss them completely; all of them eventually ran out of fuel and either made forced landings on Midway or ditched. The torpedo squadron from the *Hornet*, however, had ignored their orders and set off on their own course; at 0925 hours they spotted smoke from the Japanese ships and swooped down to attack in the face of heavy anti-aircraft fire and a large number of Zeros. Without air cover they had no chance – all 15 planes were shot down and 29 of the 30 crew were killed. At 0930 the 14 torpedo bombers from the *Enterprise* arrived, also without fighter cover; ten were shot down and the remaining four were so badly battered they could hardly make their escape. At 1000 hours Torpedo 3 from the *Yorktown* arrived with six Wildcats, which were quickly driven off by about 15 Zeros in the only fighter plane action to take place over the Japanese fleet. Only five of the 12 torpedo planes and three of the Wildcats survived the attack. No hits had been registered by the 47 aircraft, only six of which returned.

Meanwhile, 37 dive bombers from the *Enterprise* had been searching vainly for the Japanese force when the leader of the Wildcat fighter squadron radioed that he was over the enemy fleet, but that he was short on fuel and was heading home. This was the first news that Spruance and Browning had had of their strike, and Lieutenant Commander Clarence McClusky, leader of the squadron, could hear Browning screaming, 'Attack! Attack!' over the radio. Replying 'Wilco, as soon as I find the bastards,' he headed toward the carriers. At 1002 hours the dive bombers raced down from 14,000 feet toward the *Akagi* and *Kaga*.

The Japanese ships had been forced to take violet evasive maneuvers to escape the torpedo attacks and had not been able to launch more defensive fighters, while those already in the air were at a low altitude and could not climb high enough in time to meet this new attack. The *Akagi*, with 40 planes refueling on deck, sustained three hits within two minutes; one of the bombs fell on a hangar containing stored torpedoes and another struck the fueling planes on the flight deck. At 1047 hours Nagumo reluctantly transferred his flag to the light cruiser, *Nagara*; by 1915 hours that evening the fiercely burning carrier had been abandoned. The *Kaga* took four hits; one killed everyone on the bridge, including the captain, while others started fires in the bomb and gasoline storage areas. She, too, was soon abandoned and sank at 1925 hours.

While the planes from the *Enterprise* were attacking *Akagi* and *Kaga*, 17 dive bombers from *Yorktown* were swooping down to the *Soryu*. Despite starting out nearly an hour and a half later than the other attack groups, they had arrived at the same time, thanks to smart navigating advice from Hubie Strange (the weather-

man) and Oscar Pederson (the air group commander) aboard *Yorktown*. Attacking in three waves at one-minute intervals, they dropped three 1000 lb bombs on *Soryu*'s flight deck. The ship burst into flames and had to be abandoned within twenty minutes. Damage control parties had the fires under control by 1145 hours, but then the submarine *Nautilus* re-entered the fray and put three torpedoes into the carrier, restarting the fires. At 1610 hours the *Soryu* broke in half and slipped beneath the waves.

After the attacks the dive bombers headed back to their carriers. Most made it – some on literally their last gallon of gasoline – but a few had to ditch, owing to a miscalculation of the carriers' position. Three Japanese carriers had been left in flames, but the *Enterprise* had lost 14 of 37 dive bombers, ten of 14 torpedo bombers, and one Wildcat. The *Hornet* had lost all her torpedo bombers and 12 Wildcats, while her dive

BELOW: *The Japanese heavy cruiser* Mikuma *abandoned and sinking after American air attack, Midway, 6 June 1942.*

bombers had missed the battle entirely. *Yorktown* was down to seven of 12 torpedo bombers, two dive bombers, and three Wildcats. Fletcher launched a search mission to find the fourth carrier; the *Hiryu* had been far ahead of the other three carriers, and had been missed so far.

Since he still had *Hiryu*, with a full complement of planes, Nagumo decided to carry on the battle, reasoning that the Americans had only one or two carriers which had already lost most of their planes. He sent a message to Yamamoto: 'Sighted enemy composed of one carrier, five cruisers, and six destroyers at position bearing ten degrees 240 miles from Midway,' then he headed for the *Yorktown*.

The first Japanese attack group, composed of 18 Vals and six Zeros, was launched at 1100 hours, followed by a second group of ten Kates and six Zeros at 1331 hours. At the same time Admiral Kondo, who had intercepted the message to Yamamoto, signaled that he was coming north to support the carrier force, while Yamamoto ordered the light carriers *Ryujo* and *Junyo* south from the Aleutians to help.

By flying low, the Japanese planes managed to stay under the straight line beam of the *Yorktown's* crude radar, and were not detected until they were only 46 miles from the ship. At noon the carrier began taking evasive action; the heavy cruisers *Astoria* and *Portland*, as well as the destroyers *Hammann*, *Anderson*, *Russell*, *Morris*, and *Hughes*, formed a defensive ring around her; the 12 Wildcats that were airborne as combat air patrol went out to intercept, joined by several Wildcats rushed over from *Hornet*. The first wave of 24 Japanese planes arrived at 1210 hours. In a dogfight to end all dogfights, the interceptors knocked out ten Vals and three fighters, while anti-aircraft fire accounted for two more dive bombers. But three of the remaining six planes managed to score a hit. The first bomb damaged the boilers, the second started a fire that was put out by flooding, and the third exploded on the flight deck, resulting in another fire and many casualties. Fletcher transferred his flag to the *Astoria*, since *Yorktown's* communications equipment had been knocked out; but by 1340 hours repair parties had the carrier running at 18 knots again. The fighters were on deck refueling at 1630 hours when the second attack group was picked up on the radar. There were 12 Wildcats on combat air patrol, but the Kates and Zeros slipped by them and scored two torpedo hits which ruptured most of the fuel tanks on the port side, cut off all power, jammed the rudder, and caused a 17-degree list. Afraid that the *Yorktown* would capsize, and unable to repair the

damage, Captain Elliott Buckmaster gave the order to abandon ship at 1500 hours.

'Old Yorky' stayed afloat, however, and on 6 June Fletcher sent a salvage party over on the destroyer *Hammann* to attempt to get her back to port. But the *Yorktown* had been sighted by a Japanese reconnaissance plane, and the submarine *I-168* put one torpedo into *Hammann*, which sank within four minutes, and two more into the *Yorktown* before escaping through a heavy depth charge attack to wind up what had been one of the greatest submarine exploits of the war. The *Yorktown* finally sank at 0500 hours on 7 June.

The *Hiryu* was finally spotted by one of the planes Fletcher had sent out just prior to the attack on the *Yorktown* and at 1630 hours 24 dive bombers, including ten refugees from the *Yorktown*, took off from *Enterprise* – without fighter cover, since all operational Wildcats were flying defensive formations. The group found the *Hiryu* at 1700 hours and scored four solid hits, losing only three of their number. B-17s from Midway made another attack about an hour later, but made no hits. Another group of five

ABOVE AND RIGHT: *Further scenes of the damaged* Yorktown *at Midway.*

RIGHT: Yorktown *on fire after being hit by the first Japanese attack.*

Vindicators and six dive bombers took off from Midway at 1900 hours, but could not locate the carrier. The *Hiryu* was abandoned by all hands except her captain at 0230 hours the next morning, and finally sank at 0900 hours.

For all intents and purposes, the Battle of Midway was over. Yamamoto, who had been several hundred miles northwest of Nagumo during the carrier battle of 4 June, considered joining up with Kondo's Midway Occupation Force and the Aleutian force and attempting to engage the Americans in a traditional gun battle. Nagumo, who disagreed, was summarily relieved of command. But as reports came in revealing that the Americans still had two operational carriers, while all four Japanese carriers were either sunk or abandoned, Yamamoto realized that a dawn air attack was more probable than a night gun battle. He therefore reluctantly ordered his forces to turn west.

Spruance, meanwhile, had quite rightly decided that a night engagement with a large Japanese force, far better equipped than he for night fighting, would not be to his advantage. He turned east and headed away from the battle area until midnight.

Midway was the first defeat ever suffered by the Japanese Navy, and news of the debacle was completely suppressed in Japan. All papers concerning the event were classified top secret and destroyed in 1945, so that the Japanese public

LEFT: *A destroyer comes alongside the* Lexington *to rescue crew during the Battle of the Coral Sea.*

BELOW: *A damaged Avenger bomber on Midway Island after the battle.*

only learned of the events at Midway in the 1950s when published accounts began to appear.

Japan lost four large carriers, one heavy cruiser, 322 planes, and 3500 men at Midway, against one large carrier, 150 planes, and 307 men for the Americans. Though Yamamoto blamed the disaster on the failure of his advance screen of submarines to locate and harass the Americans, in fact the responsibility for deploying the submarines in the wrong place was his. It was also Yamamoto who divided his huge fleet and then devised for it a rigid, highly complicated battle plan that was entirely based on what he assumed the Americans would do. The Americans did not follow the script, and the Japanese commanders were not trained to adapt rapidly to radically different situations.

But without the complete and accurate intelligence reports gathered by the Americans, the Japanese plan might well have succeeded. These reports, which gave Nimitz the time and knowledge to dispose his forces correctly, were probably the crucial factor in the victory.

The Battle of Midway is worthy of note in the history of naval warfare, in that it marks the end of the transition period between the eras dominated by battleships and by carriers. Even more than Coral Sea, Midway demonstrated the central role of the carrier plane. Despite a fleet that remained largely intact and immeasurably superior gun power, Yamamoto was forced to retire without firing a shot once he lost his air cover.

Midway saw the debut of the Zeke, or Zero-3 fighter plane. The original Zero had been far more maneuverable and had a rate of climb three times greater than its American counterparts, and the new Zero was a vast improvement. But the Japanese pilots proved to be inferior to the Americans, an indication of the deterioration of the Japanese air arm and the growing shortage of well-trained pilots since Pearl Harbor. On the American side, the Dauntless dive bomber, which was to become the most successful carrier plane of the war, performed superbly, while the Devastator torpedo bomber proved so disappointing that it was taken off the list of naval combat planes and replaced by the new Avenger.

The Battle of Midway did not decide the entire course of the Pacific War in a moment, nor did it end with the utter destruction of one of the combatants. Its importance lies in the fact that it broke Japan's naval superiority and restored the balance between the two navies. Once that had happened, as Yamamoto foresaw, it was only a matter of time until economic mobilization allowed America to overwhelm Japan.

4.
The American Advance Begins

Immediately after the Battle of Midway, the focus of the war in the Pacific moved back to the Southwest Pacific Area. The failure at Midway had squandered the margin of naval strength that Admiral Yamamoto had gained for Japan at Pearl Harbor and restored the balance between the Japanese and American navies. Many of the Japanese generals therefore believed that now the offensive should be limited, that over-long lines of communication should be avoided, that combat should be declined whenever possible, and that Japan should not be drawn into a debilitating contest for islands of marginal strategic use. But contrary to the views of its sister service and despite the fact that the loss of its carriers had condemned it to fight a defensive war, the Navy resolved to defend its heavy commitments in the Southwest Pacific, first by enlarging its position and subsequently by selling its territory inch by bloody inch in the hope that the United States would weary of the attack. Thus the initial occupation of Tulagi was to grow into the Guadalcanal campaign while a new assault against Port Moresby was launched overland.

The Japanese Navy was opposed in these objectives by an enemy with a command divided between a general and an admiral. Escaping by submarine after his defeat in the Philippines, General Douglas MacArthur had arrived in Australia in March to assume command of the Southwest Pacific Theater. MacArthur found his new command short of manpower, poorly equipped, and quite deficient in air power. He also found Australian morale shattered by the Allied débâcle in Asia and especially by the fall of Singapore which had been regarded by the Australians as the keystone of their security. MacArthur made the reconquest of Papua his first priority, as it was from Papua that the Japanese posed the most immediate threat to Australia, the main American base in the South Pacific.

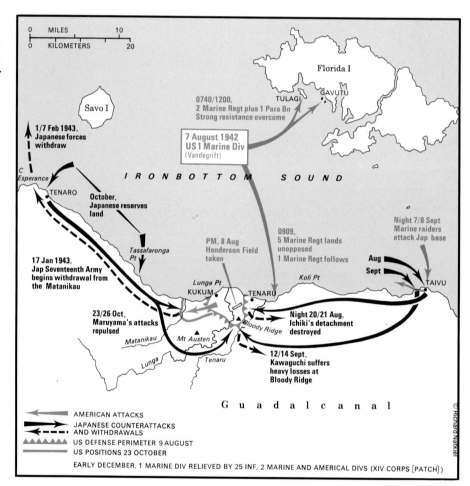

Since a large part of New Guinea was Australian territory, a strong offensive there would do wonders for Australian morale. Perceived by both the Japanese and their opponent as a primary objective, New Guinea was to be the scene of a hard fought campaign.

The other Allied command sector was the Central Pacific Theater of Admiral Chester Nimitz, based in Hawaii. He was often in conflict with MacArthur over strategy and priorities. Nimitz represented the overall desire of the American Navy to fight a war of ships and planes in the vast expanses of the Pacific Ocean to the exclusion of the Army whenever possible.

ABOVE: *The land fighting on Guadalcanal.*

RIGHT: *Events during the Naval Battle of Guadalcanal on the night of 14/15 November.*

ABOVE RIGHT:
General Hyakutake
commanded the
Japanese 17th Army
based in Rabaul with
overall responsibility
for Guadalcanal.

ABOVE: *Japanese*
installations on
Gavutu island burn
following US air
attacks.

Although MacArthur was in conflict with the Army chiefs in Washington over the global priorities of the war, he did represent the interest of the Army against the Navy in this inter-service rivalry.

The sudden shift in the fortunes of the Japanese after Midway brought the same desire to both MacArthur and Nimitz – to go on the offensive as quickly as possible. The prospective offensive raised intense and indeed passionate debate about command arrangements, but a compromise was reached. Nimitz was to direct initial operations in the eastern Solomons,

beginning with Tulagi and Guadalcanal. Subsequent operations by MacArthur were to clear the northern coast of New Guinea and capture Rabaul, the main Japanese base in the Southwest Pacific, and the remainder of the Bismarck Archipelago. 'Operation Watchtower' was the name given to the offensive.

On 5 July 1942 reconnaissance aircraft confirmed the reports of the Australian coastwatchers that the Japanese had transferred large troop concentrations from Tulagi to the nearby island of Guadalcanal, and were building an airfield of unknown proportions. This news threw a monkeywrench into the entire operation for, if the Japanese were allowed to complete an airfield unopposed, they would be able to launch fighters and bombers at all Allied attempts to move into the Solomons and the Coral Sea. The all-important objective was now to seize Guadalcanal and the strategic airstrip at Lunga Point, later to be renamed Henderson Field, and consequently the Santa Cruz portion was dropped from the agenda.

Guadalcanal was no paradise as the Marines who fought and died there knew well. It was a hell hole, an island forgotten in time. Ninety miles long and 25 miles wide, a mixture of rain forests, stinking malarial swamps, thick grass-

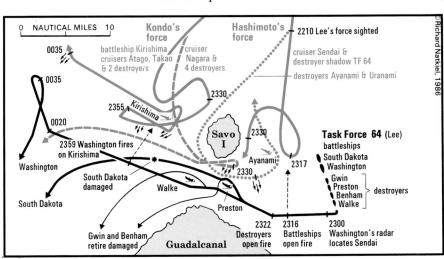

LEFT: *Gun crew aboard the carrier* Wasp *snatch a hurried meal during operations off Guadalcanal in early August 1942.*

RIGHT: *A Japanese naval landing force machine gun crew seen in a photograph taken from a captured Japanese on Guadalcanal in 1942.*

lands and undergrowth, and steep, treacherous mountains; that was Guadalcanal, a strategic objective for a few months on a general's map which later as the war progressed would be forgotten and returned to its semi-primeval state of existence. 'The Canal', as it became known to the Marines who fought on it and to the American people who read about it in their daily papers, was situated in the southern half of the Solomons group, which runs for 600 miles in a southeast direction from Rabaul, Buka and Bougainville. The remaining islands and atolls form a double chain separated by a deep channel which was given the name of 'The Slot'.

In the weeks which followed, plans were thrashed out, differences settled, troops gathered and an overall strategic commander selected, Vice-Admiral Robert Ghormley. The amphibious force was commanded by Rear Admiral Richard Kelly Turner. Rear Admiral Frank Fletcher, who commanded the carrier task force at the Battles of the Coral Sea and Midway, was in command of the carriers off Guadalcanal and provided air cover for the operation. The air support force was composed of the carriers *Enterprise*, *Saratoga* and *Wasp*

RIGHT: *Japanese transport ships beached on Guadalcanal burn in the background, 16 November 1942.*

LEFT: *Admiral McCain (right) at an American base in the Solomons in 1942.*

screened by the new battleship *North Carolina*, six cruisers and 16 destroyers. The convoy of transports consisted of four cruisers and 11 destroyers, and was to carry the 1st US Marine Division. The Marine force was commanded by a crusty old fighter, Major General Alexander Archer Vandegrift. The convoy was screened by Rear Admiral Victor Crutchley with a force of three Australian and two American cruisers (HMAS *Australia*, *Canberra* and *Hobart*, USS *Chicago* and USS *San Juan*).

The operation was being supported by land-based aircraft from airfields in Fiji, New Caledonia and the New Hebrides, and also by army aircraft under MacArthur's command. There were to be two landings, the first on the larger island of Guadalcanal and the second on the much smaller island of Tulagi.

Although these preparations seemed quite thorough, in fact, the organization behind the operation left much to be desired. Vandegrift had been given very little time to train his men and get them acclimatized. Although the 1st Marine Division had a core of seasoned veterans, most of the men were new recruits with no fighting experience. The operation was nicknamed 'Operation Shoestring' because it had been so hastily put together. Vandegrift pushed the target date back by a week for a landing on 7 August but could not get a further extension. Thus much equipment and materiel was left on the docks at Wellington, New Zealand. The amphibious force set off on 22nd July and met the air support task force south of Fiji: after a four-day practice on a remote island of the group, they set sail for the 'Canal' on 31 July. The force was undetected in its approach because of heavy haze and intermittent rain squalls. On 7 August the initial landings were made on Red Beach at Guadalcanal near Lunga Point and on Tulagi. There was no opposition on Guadalcanal as all the Japanese technicians had fled into the jungle and by nightfall 11,000 Marines were ashore. On the next day, the airfield was secured and the Marines put out scouts to ascertain what the Japanese were planning. On Tulagi the situation was not as clear-cut, the Japanese were better prepared, and the three battalions of Marines met stiff resistance. By 8 August Tulagi was completely under Marine control, the casualties were 108 Marines dead and 140 wounded. The Japanese garrison of 1500 troops was practically exterminated to a man. Meanwhile, it had taken only 48 hours to gain the initial foothold on the 'Canal,' but it would be another six months of intense and bitter fighting before it could be secured. The scene was now set for one of the cruellest, hardest fought campaigns in the Pacific.

When the news of the landings reached Rabaul, Admiral Mikawa Gunichi was in the middle of preparing for a major offensive against Port Moresby. He immediately guessed American intentions and decided to send all available ships to attack and destroy the US naval forces off Guadalcanal, and then to exterminate the Marine landing force on the island. By 7 August, five heavy and two light cruisers were sailing toward the 'Canal.' To make matters worse, Imperial General Headquarters issued orders to reinforce the garrison of the island and a convoy carrying 500 additional troops, with a destroyer escort was also *en route*. But shortly after setting sail one of the transports was torpedoed by an American submarine, so the convoy was recalled to Rabaul.

On the beach itself, the supply and logistics problems were mounting for Vandegrift, who was trying to keep to his original timetable. At 1400 hours, he ordered the 1st Battalion, 5th Marines to advance westward to Alligator Creek and dig in for the night. By 1600 hours Vandegrift was ashore and had established his for-

LEFT: *Part of the American transport fleet photographed from the cruiser* Chicago *off Tulagi on 10 August.*

BELOW: *Japanese Betty bombers make a low level attack on the US supply ships off Guadalcanal.*

ward command post. During all this the Japanese were far from idle, they had launched two air strikes. The first was at 1320 hours and consisted of 24 aircraft of the Japanese 25th Air Flotilla. Warning was received from an Australian coastwatcher and a welcoming party was arranged. Twelve Japanese aircraft were shot down by Wildcats from the *Saratoga*, but the USS *Mugford*, a destroyer, was hit and 22 men killed. Two hours later there was an attack by ten dive bombers but no serious damage was recorded. The First Marine combat group, commanded by Colonel Clifton Cates, had been ordered by Vandegrift to proceed to Mount Austen but they were held up by the terrific heat and tropical undergrowth. Vandegrift realized that Mount Austen would not be reached that day; so he changed his plans accordingly. The Marines were to secure their positions and dig in for the night. The next morning the Marines would push forward toward the Lunga and bypass Mount Austen, occupying the airstrip from the south. The 5th Marines were to advance on Lunga also and then continue to Kukum. There were many shaky Marines on the first night but the Japanese did not make the expected counterattack. On Saturday, 8 August, the 1st Battalion, 5th Marines, supported by the 1st Tank Battalion, succeeded in crossing the mouth of Alligator Creek. The Marines believed that this was in fact the Tenaru River, but it was in reality the Ilu. The 1st Battalion, 1st Marines, acting on orders swung west away from Mount Austen and began to advance. This unit moved very slowly and had difficulty crossing one of the numerous creeks in its path. The other units, the 2nd and 3rd Battalions made faster progress through the jungle than their counterparts in the 1st. The day was extremely hot and humid to say the least and by the end of the day the 1st Battalion had passed the airfield, but the 2nd and 3rd Battalions had in their turn slowed down and were still south of the airfield when the order came to dig in.

The 5th Marines made good progress and managed to take a few Japanese prisoners. It was gathered from information sweated out of the enemy that no Japanese resistance would be encountered within the next 48 hours. Vandegrift took immediate advantage of this situation and ordered the 5th Marines to advance more rapidly. The regiment crossed the Lunga over the main bridge, and by skirting the airfield to the north, it took Kukum along with large quantities of supplies.

Meanwhile the situation on the beach was not going according to plan and after another attack by Japanese Betty bombers escorted by Zero fighters, Fletcher's fighter strength was being gradually thinned down. From 99 aircraft, he was now down to 78 and was also dangerously low on fuel reserves. Fletcher decided that he was putting his entire Task Force 61 in jeopardy if he remained off Guadalcanal any longer and asked Ghormley for permission to withdraw his carriers. Ghormley was not too happy with this but because he was too far removed from the scene felt that it would be unreasonable to deny such an urgent request. This decision was the most controversial made during the entire Guadalcanal campaign; the main points being that only 50 percent of the supplies for the Marine force had been unloaded; Fletcher still had enough fuel for at least 72 hours and the Japanese air attacks had been beaten off; and the majority of ships were undamaged. However, Mikawa's force was steaming down the Slot making for Guadalcanal. US aircraft had sighted the Japanese squadron on the evening of 7 August but due to a belated report giving the wrong information, and bad weather, the enemy was not located again. Therefore, Mikawa was able to make his approach undetected.

Turner summoned Rear Admiral Crutchley and Major General Vandegrift aboard his flagship the USS *McCawley*, and relayed the information to them that Fletcher was pulling out and taking their air cover and supplies with him.

Vandegrift's response to this was not recorded, but he must have been very angry. While Turner was expanding on the details, Mikawa's force sailed right past the picket destroyers and turned their guns to bear point blank at the unsuspecting *Canberra* and *Chicago*. The *Canberra* was hit so hard that she had to be abandoned but the *Chicago* was more fortunate, and received no crippling damage. The Japanese did not wait to see the result of their surprise attack but sailed out of range and toward the northern patrol group. The southern patrol group was so confused that no warning was sent to the northern group. The northern group fared worse that its southern counterparts. The Japanese sank the USS *Astoria*, *Vincennes* and *Quincy* in less than an hour. Mikawa had taken the US Navy by surprise and the result was an astounding victory which would have been even more resounding if he had taken the initiative and destroyed the unprotected transports. It is only conjecture but the entire campaign would have changed, and possibly the war in the Pacific taken a different turn if the transports had been eliminated.

This disaster, and disaster is exactly what it was, confirmed Fletcher's belief that he must remove his task force from the danger zone. The 9 August was spent in preparation for departure and by sunset Task Force 61 was steaming away. The Marines under Vandegrift were now com-

ABOVE & LEFT: *Two views of Japanese attacks hitting home on the carrier* Hornet *during the Battle of Santa Cruz, 26 October 1942. The* Hornet *sank later.*

RIGHT: *Also sunk during the Guadalcanal campaign was the carrier* Wasp, *this time by the Japanese submarine* I-19 *on 15 September.*

pletely on their own. The situation was not very inviting. The US Navy had lost control of the seas around the Solomons. The nearest air support was in Espiritu Santo in the New Hebrides. Supplies were already beginning to run out, and morale was not very high after what most Marines thought was naval desertion. Vandegrift realized that he was in no position to attack, so his schedule stressed defense. His most important operational concern was to make the airstrip functional at all costs. An extended perimeter defense was established around the airfield. The Marines set up .30 and .50 caliber machineguns, backed up by 37 mm guns and 90 mm AA guns all around the defensive perimeter. The feeling of being abandoned was considerably lessened on 14 August when the Navy ran the gauntlet of enemy aircraft and surface ships to bring supplies of ammunition and fuel, as well as the bare essentials to the Marines at Guadalcanal. Vandegrift decided to make a small foray against the Japanese by driving them back across

the Matanikau River. This action was successful but did not allay the doubts in his mind of the ability of his men to sustain and repulse a heavy attack from the numerically superior Japanese force assembling on the island. The major thing which aided the Marines was the Japanese confusion over exactly what to do – the Japanese believed that the US would eventually get tired of the 'insignificant' island and withdraw. Japanese intelligence showed, however, that the Marines were digging in and this put a whole new picture on the screen. Plans were made to expel the Marines from Guadalcanal. Lieutenant General Hyakutake Haruyoshi, 17th Army Commander was ordered to retake Tulagi and Guadalcanal before setting out on the all important mission of securing Port Moresby. Hyakutake had over 50,000 men in his 17th Army but they were spread out all over the south Pacific. Undaunted, he believed that, if he could send one really crack unit into the islands, the Marine force could be driven into the sea and utterly

ABOVE: *Marines put out fire on a Grumman Wildcat fighter following a Japanese air attack on Henderson Field, December 1942.*

destroyed. He chose Colonel Ichiki Kiyanao's 28th Infantry from Guam to accomplish the task. At the time, he appeared to be the ideal man for the task at hand but events proved him to be impetuous and rash. On 18 August he was to take 900 men of six destroyers and land at Taivu Point, around 20 miles from the Marine positions. The remainder of his 2500-man outfit would join him within the week.

Vandegrift was being kept up to date by his native coastwatchers and knew that Japanese forces were building up in the east. Captain Charles Brush set out on a patrol on 19 August with Marines of Able Company, 1st Marines and headed toward Koli Point. At noon Japanese troops were sighted, Brush sent his executive officer, Lieutenant Joseph Jachym round to flank them and put them in a cross-fire between the two marine columns. The result was 31 out of 35 Japanese dead. From the documents and maps taken from the bodies it was discovered that they were army personnel and not navy men who had

previously been fighting the Marines on Guadalcanal.

Ichiki attacked the Marine positions on the mouth of Alligator Creek on the Ilu River (still called the Tenaru by the US), early on 21 August. He recklessly decided that the 900 men he had brought with him would be sufficient and he need not wait for the rest of his 2500-man force. The Japanese made two attempts: the first at 0240 hours and the second at 0500 hours, both attacks were repulsed with heavy casualties to the attackers. Some of the Japanese were caught on the far bank of the river and Colonel Gerald Thomas, Divisional Operations Officer, recommended to Vandegrift to counterattack immediately and drive the survivors into the sea. Vandegrift ordered the reserve battalion, 1st Battalion, 1st Marines under Lieutenant Colonel Creswell to cross the river and drive all Japanese troops downstream. Meanwhile Pollock's men provided a heavy and continuous fire from the other side of the river. Also, to insure total suc-

ABOVE: *Five brothers named Sullivan served aboard the cruiser* Juneau *and all were killed when the ship was sunk in November 1942. A destroyer was named USS* The Sullivans *in their memory later in the war and regulations were introduced to prevent a similar tragedy by stopping close relatives serving together.*

ABOVE LEFT & LEFT: *Two views of closely-packed Japanese casualties on Guadalcanal show the lack of sophistication in Japanese tactics.*

cess, a platoon of light tanks was brought up and Marine aircraft would be utilized to strafe the entire affected area. Needless to say, the operation was a complete success. In Vandegrift's own words, 'the rear of the tanks looked like meat grinders.' By 1700 hours the Battle of Tenaru (Ilu) was finished. The Marines had killed over 800 Japanese, taken 15 prisoners and of the survivors, most of these died in the jungle. Colonel Ichiki survived the battle but upon reaching Taivu, he shot himself after burning his regimental colors.

The Battle of Tenaru was an American victory but there was still a great deal to be done before Vandegrift's position on Guadalcanal could be called secure. The Japanese became even more determined than ever to drive the Marines off the island. To make the airfield serviceable, US Marine Corps engineers used captured Japanese equipment, as their own was still on board the transports. On 12 August the aide to Rear Admiral John McCain flew a Catalina flying boat onto the airfield for an inspection of the runway. McCain was responsible for land-based air operations. The strip was only 2600 ft long, with no drainage and no steel matting coverage, and finally there were no taxiways. The aide was a

realistic man and passed the field as fit for fighter aircraft operations. The airfield was named Henderson Field after a hero of the Battle of Midway. The first aircraft arrived on 20 August; 12 Dauntless dive bombers commanded by Major Richard Mangrum and 19 Marine Wildcat fighters under Captain John Smith.

Dogfights were now a matter of daily routine for the Marines. But without these pilots and the support crews of the 'Cactus Air Force' as it became known, Vandegrift's Marines might not have held their beachhead in the black days of August and September 1942. These Marine pilots lived in tents and dug-outs, their stable diet was rice and spam but they were the actual front line of resistance at the 'Canal.' Still, at the beginning of September, Vandegrift's position was not very reassuring to say the least. His battle-weary troops were hungry, stricken with dysentery and jungle rot and by October malaria would also take its toll. The Marines could not get an uninterrupted night's sleep because of the Japanese night prowler aircraft nicknamed 'Louis the Louse' and 'Washing Machine Charlie.' Morale in the American camp was falling. Tension mounted as the Americans had to wait for the Japanese to act.

Although American air power enabled the Allies to dominate the waters around Guadalcanal by day, the Japanese ruled at night, when ships from Rabaul ran fresh troops, ammunition and food into Guadalcanal and bombarded the airfield, renamed Henderson Field. Known as the 'Tokyo Express' these fast convoys were conducted with great audacity by Rear Admiral Tanaka Raizo.

On 23 August the American Task Force 61, including the carriers *Enterprise*, *Saratoga* and *Wasp* under the command of Vice Admiral Frank Fletcher, intercepted an attempt to run supplies to Guadalcanal in daylight. The Japanese transports were supported by a Striking Force under Admiral Nagumo, with the carriers *Shokaku* and *Zuikaku* and a diversionary group based on the small carrier *Ryujo*.

The first American strike on 23 August was avoided by a reversal of course but next day search aircraft found the *Ryujo* and a strike was launched. An attempt to divert the strike to the bigger carriers which were located after the aircraft took off was frustrated by communications problems, and only a few aircraft from the *Enterprise* were able to attack the *Shokaku*, but the

ABOVE: *Admiral Yamamoto.*

ABOVE LEFT: *Navy Secretary Forrestal (second left) during a tour of inspection in the Solomons.*

LEFT: *America's top military men for most of World War II. From left, General Arnold, USAAF Chief of Staff, Admiral Leahy, Chief of Staff to the President, Admiral King, Navy Chief of Staff, and General Marshall, Army Chief of Staff.*

urgent requests was granted; the Cactus Air Force was down to only 11 out of 38 Wildcats, and Ghormley sent an immediate 24 replacements. Colonel Edson moved his command post and his mixed force of Raiders and Parachutists to a ridge one mile south of Henderson Field and not far from Vandegrift's own headquarters. This ridge was 1000 yards long, running northwest to southeast, and surrounded by steep undulating thick jungle growth. This was to be renamed Bloody Ridge in a few days.

Edson deployed his 700 men in the prime locations for a possible Japanese penetration attempt. The jungle was cleared and barbed wire strung out between the trees to give it the appearance of a perimeter. In direct support of Edson's men were 105mm howitzers and the 2nd Battalion, 5th Marines. On 12 September the long-awaited Japanese attack was at last launched. It started off with an intense naval bombardment of the Marine positions, followed up immediately by heavy mortar and artillery fire and then an all-out infantry attack by Kawaguchi's troops. The Marines were displaced from their positions but through faulty communications and the disorientation of their men, the Japanese attack lost impetus and stopped. The Marines under Edson then charged and retook their former positions along the ridge. Now started the long process of redigging in, laying more barbed wire and getting ready for the next attack which would surely come. The noise was intense, again naval bombardment, artillery and mortar barrages and the follow-up by infantry. Kawaguchi threw 2000 men across the slope on 13 September. This mass wave of men was something which the Marines had never experienced before, as fast as they cut them down, their comrades just climbed over the dead bodies. The Marines were at the breaking point when 'Red Mike' Edson took the front himself and urged his weary men to smoke down all the enemy. Edson called for increased artillery support and practically brought it down to his own positions. Another stalwart was Major Kenneth Bailey who kept screaming at the top of his lungs the traditional Marine Corps cry 'Do you want to live forever.' Between the intense and accurate fire coming from the Marines on the ridge and the perfect artillery support, the Japanese were being decimated. By 14 September the Japanese were defeated and Kawaguchi knew it. The remainder of his force were retreating to the Matanikau. The result of Bloody Ridge was an ocean of dead and wounded. Japanese dead totaled over 700 with an additional 600 wounded. The US casualties were 59 dead and 204 wounded.

Ryujo was sunk at 1550. Nearly an hour later the main Japanese carrier air group retaliated by inflicting severe damage on the *Enterprise*, and both carrier task forces retired to lick their wounds, leaving Rear Admiral Tanaka's Transport Group to continue on its way.

Tanaka's force was badly mauled next day by shore-based aircraft, and as a result the Tokyo Express was forced to resume night operations. Daylight operations were impossible in the face of American air superiority won by the pilots of the Cactus Air Force.

Vandegrift was still in desperate need of reinforcements with the Japanese landing more and more troops both to the east and west of his perimeter. He transferred troops from Tulagi to Guadalcanal, including the experienced Edson's Raiders. The Marines made occasional thrusts into the Japanese held areas to keep the enemy on their toes and to gather intelligence information. On 10 September, one of Vandegrift's

The US Marines had won another total victory but this was to be over-shadowed again by a defeat at sea.

Admiral Turner was keeping his word and rushing reinforcements to Guadalcanal. These were the 7th Marines which he had picked up at the New Hebrides after their stint of duty on Samoa. The task force and its carrier escort force was sighted on 14 September by a Japanese aircraft. Turner remained on course until nightfall and then withdrew *McCawley* and the six precious transports and its cargo of 4000 Marines. The carriers *Hornet* and *Wasp*, the battleship *North Carolina* and various destroyers continued on course. On 15 September, at 0220 hours, the Japanese submarines *I-15* and *I-19* attacked the carrier force. The result of this attack as devastating: the *Wasp* was abandoned and sunk by the *Lansdowne*, *North Carolina* had a 30 by 18 ft gaping hole put in its side below the waterline and the destroyer *O'Brien* was also sunk. This naval action was off the Santa Cruz islands and again the US Navy had suffered another blow by

ABOVE: *General Marshall and Secretary of War Henry Stimson confer.*

LEFT: *General MacArthur inspecting an Australian unit.*

ABOVE RIGHT: *One of the first setbacks that the Japanese received on land was in fighting at Milne Bay in northeast New Guinea where this Australian soldier is shown with a destroyed Japanese tank.*

RIGHT: *US tanks and infantry co-operate against Japanese infiltrators during the fighting on Bougainville.*

the Imperial Navy. Turner's decision temporarily to withdraw the transports was vindicated by their safe arrival at Guadalcanal and the landing of the 4000 men and some supplies.

On the night of 11-12 October 1942 the Americans tried their own version of the Tokyo Express, with a supply convoy to Guadalcanal, and a night action ensued off Cape Esperance. The US covering force, Task Force 64 under Rear Admiral Norman Scott, ran into a similar force under Rear Admiral Goto, but a sighting by the light cruiser *Helena* was not passed to Scott, who assumed he had missed the enemy. While the Americans were reversing course, the Japanese were detected by the destroyer *Duncan*, which opened fire independently, but the US cruisers did not join in the firing until 2346. In the confused fighting which followed the heavy cruiser *Furutaka* and the destroyer *Fubuki* were sunk, in return for only one destroyer, the USS *Duncan*. Unfortunately for the Americans they believed that they had mastered the Japanese in the art of night-fighting.

The Japanese command planned a new land offensive on Guadalcanal and this began on 21 October. Substantial naval forces were sent to support the attack with the four carriers being ordered to send their aircraft to Henderson Field once it had been captured from the defending US Marines. In the event the Marines' defense proved too strong for the Japanese land forces and at sea a major naval battle, the Battle of Santa Cruz, developed. Although the Japanese had four carriers with 212 planes to the Americans' two carriers and 171 planes the result was by no means a clear victory. Although the *Hornet* was sunk and the *Enterprise* badly damaged in return for two Japanese carriers hit, Japanese losses in aircrew left their surviving ships crippled and they, like the Americans, had to withdraw.

There was then a brief lull in the fighting while both sides experimented and probed the enemy's defensive positions. The Marines lost a few skirmishes and won a few but it was not until November that the next offensive really got under way. The US was determined not to lose its hold on Guadalcanal. As the struggle reached

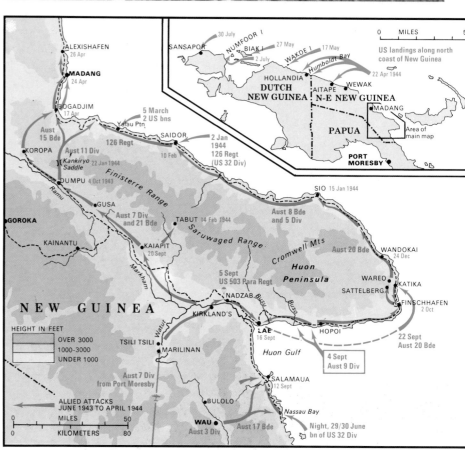

ABOVE: *Vehicles come ashore from landing ships on an island in the Southwest Pacific.*

ABOVE LEFT: *Jungle fighting on New Guinea.*

LEFT: *The developments in the Allied offensive in New Guinea in 1943-44 with, inset, the later Allied landings.*

its climax, President Roosevelt ordered the Chiefs of Staff to send all available equipment, supplies and troops to the two priority theaters – the South Pacific and North Africa – even if this meant drastically reducing commitments elsewhere. Admiral King, CNO, could not send any carriers but he diverted a sizeable force nonetheless, including a battleship, six cruisers, 24 submarines and 130 naval aircraft. General George Marshall, Army Chief of Staff, also sent an additional 75 army aircraft from Hawaii but would not increase the troop commitment to the area, especially with the pressure on from Operation Torch, the Allied landings in North Africa. However, reinforcements were stripped from the other island bases and sent to the 'Canal.' On 4 November two regiments from the 2nd Marine Division were landed and a further 6000 officers and men were landed on 6 November from Noumea and Espiritu Santo (the latter were troops of the Americal Division). The two convoys were commanded by Rear Admiral Turner, and were escorted by two squadrons, the first under Rear Admiral Nicholas Scott and the second under Rear Admiral Daniel Callaghan. This force was

shadowed by a task force formed around the hastily refitted *Enterprise* and the two battleships *Washington* and *South Dakota*.

The Japanese were still no less determined than the US Marines to gain complete control over Guadalcanal, and November saw another major attempt to reinforce the island and force the Marines out once and for all. Their plan was basically no different from all previous attempts. Bombardment by two naval squadrons of Henderson Field, was to be followed up again by artillery and mortar fire and a massive infantry break-through. The only difference this time was that a third squadron was escorting the rest of the 38th Division from Rabaul, while a fourth squadron gave support. This was by far the largest planned general offensive to date.

Unknowingly, the US convoy, escorted by Rear Admiral Scott's squadron arrived off Lunga Point early on 11 November and was joined by Callaghan's squadron on 12 November. Just a few hours later, a strong Japanese naval force, including the battleships *Hiei* and *Kirishima*, was sighted steaming down the Slot. Turner calmly finished unloading the transports

of all troops and supplies and then sailed in convoy for Espiritu Santo, only escorted by three destroyers. The remainder of the combined escort forces, commanded by Rear Admiral Callaghan, stayed behind to engage the enemy fleet. Although outnumbered by superior Japanese forces, he did so to cover Turner's withdrawal.

After escorting the transports clear of the anchorage, Callaghan steered west to engage the enemy. It was an extremely dark and dismal night with no moon. In the early hours of the morning of 13 November, both forces practically collided before opening fire. The battle which followed lasted only 24 minutes and must go on record as being one of the most furious sea engagements ever fought. The Japanese lost two destroyers.

The battleship *Hiei* was critically damaged, and left dead in the water for the US aircraft to finish off the next day. The US task force lost two light cruisers and four destroyers; both Rear Admirals Callaghan and Scott were killed in the battle and casualties were heavy. Callaghan's action accomplished its main objective, however, allowing the task force time to intervene. The following afternoon, naval aircraft from the carrier *Enterprise* sank a cruiser and severely damaged other surface ships of the Japanese cruiser bombardment force. Furthermore, aircraft from Henderson Field inflicted grave damage to the transports unloading on the north side of the island and sank seven out of 11. The Japanese heavy bombardment force was now reorganized

ABOVE: *Airfield construction equipment is unloaded from an LST on Middleburg Island near New Guinea's Cape Sansapor in August 1944. Airfield construction was always a priority following any amphibious operation.*

ABOVE RIGHT:
Gunners aboard a
PT-boat fire on
Japanese positions
during the landings at
Biak in August 1944.

RIGHT: *The destroyer*
Downes *bombards*
Japanese positions on
Marcus Island,
October 1944.

ABOVE: *The crew of the destroyer O'Bannon enjoy a brief recreation in Tulagi harbor off Guadalcanal in 1943.*

and reinforced to cover the transports. It was composed of the battleship *Kirishima*, four cruisers and nine destroyers. Vice-Admiral 'Bull' Halsey, who had relieved Ghormley on 18 October, sent Rear Admiral Willis Lee with the battleships *Washington* and *South Dakota*, and four destroyers to attack it. Lee led his small squadron around the southeast tip of Guadalcanal and just after midnight engaged the enemy in the narrow channel south of Savo Island. This battle was fought at a longer range than the preceding one, but the fighting was just as intense. The *Kirishima* was so heavily damaged that she had to be scuttled; and one Japanese and three US destroyers had been sunk. The *South Dakota* was damaged but remained afloat. At daylight on 15 November, the four remaining Japanese

transports were spotted by the Marines aground and helpless; shore batteries opened up and aided by aircraft from Henderson Field turned them into blazing hulks. Out of 10,000 troops which sailed with the ill-fated expedition, only 4000 arrived and they were without equipment or rations. The three-day battle of Guadalcanal was the first decisive victory for the US Navy since the beginning of the Solomons campaign.

At the end of November the Japanese tried once more to reinforce Guadalcanal, but Halsey sent out a squadron of five cruisers and four destroyers to intercept. On 30 November, this cruiser squadron encountered eight Japanese destroyers attempting to bring supplies and reinforcements to the garrison at Tassafaronga. Only one Japanese destroyer was sunk, but the US Navy had four of its cruisers hit by torpedoes. This was the last of the midnight encounters in the narrow waters of the South Solomons. On the last day of 1942 Japanese Imperial General Headquarters decided to abandon Guadalcanal and fall back to a line of defense based on New Georgia. On 9 December General Alexander Patch relieved Vandegrift and during the next two months the 1st Marine Division was withdrawn for a much needed rest to Australia. It was relieved by the 25th US Division on 31 December. On 4 January 1943 the 2nd Marine Division headquarters and 6th Marine Regiment arrived from New Zealand, bringing the strength of the Guadalcanal garrison to 50,000 men. The Japanese on the other hand were down to 25,000 effectives. They were underfed and disease-ridden, but were still will-

ABOVE: *The heavy cruiser* Quincy *seen early in the war. The* Quincy *was sunk off Guadalcanal in the Battle of Savo Island in August 1942. A second ship of the same name entered service later in the war.*

RIGHT: *Victory markings are applied to a destroyer's gun director.*

ing to fight to the last man. General Imamura, Commander in Chief, 8th Area Army ordered them to Cape Esperance, from where they were to be evacuated during the first week in February. Exactly six months after the first US Marines landed at Red Beach on Guadalcanal, the last Japanese had been safely evacuated from the 'Canal.' General Patch was left in undisputed control of the island. This was the first US land victory achieved in World War II and marked the limits of Japanese expansion.

Even as the first shots began to rattle in the Guadalcanal campaign, a Japanese force was advancing overland in a renewed attempt on Port Moresby. The Battle of the Coral Sea in May 1942 had aborted the seaborne assault on Port Moresby, but at the same time the Japanese had established a base at Lae on the north coast of New Guinea and on 21 July landed 2000 men near Buna. By the 29th, the Japanese had seized Kokoda halfway across the island and had 13,000 men driving on Port Moresby.

Most of the Australian divisions previously serving with the British Eighth Army in North Africa had now been brought back for the defense of their country and there were eight new divisions in training. Two American divisions and eight air groups were based in Australia as well. Two Australian brigades held Port Moresby while a third was based at Milne Bay on the eastern tip of the Papuan peninsula. Two battalions had been despatched over the Kokoda trail to establish a base at Buna to cover the planned Allied attack on New Guinea. These last had collided with the Japanese force moving over the same route from the opposite direction to attack Port Moresby. The Australians had been unable to halt the Japanese advance until the fighting reached the 8500 feet-high Owen Stanley Mountains. As the Japanese attacked in very difficult terrain with lengthening supply lines, they met stiffening Australian resistance and harassment from the air. The advance was finally halted only 30 miles from its objective by an Australian division which had won distinction at El Alamein. Meanwhile, 2000 Japanese Marines nearly succeeded in capturing the airstrip at Milne Bay after five days of fierce fighting but were finally forced to re-embark by Australian troops.

By mid-September MacArthur was ready to take the offensive in Papua with the Sixth and Seventh Australian Divisions and an American regiment. Operational command was in the hands of General Sir Thomas Blamey, the Australian Commander in Chief of Allied land forces in the Southwest Pacific. Roles were now reversed as the Allied forces tried to drive the Japanese back over the route they had both so recently contested. It was at this point that Imperial General Headquarters decided to de-emphasize operations in Papua and throw all resources into the struggle for Guadalcanal. Allied progress remained slow, however, as the Japanese put up fierce resistance. The Papuan campaign was also being waged with considerable acrimony on the Allied side. The slow advance of the Australians frustrated MacArthur who considered these troops inferior to his Americans. The American troops in return received criticism from the Australians, criticism which had more than a grain of truth in it.

The Allied offensive was renewed in October, but the advance was still painfully slow in MacArthur's view, even though the Australians had reopened the Kokoda airfield by November 2, which eased Allied supply problems and enabled better air support. A Japanese stand at the Kumasi River was overcome with the assistance of air-dropped bridging materials and an airlift of troops to the north coast to threaten the Japanese flank. Falling back on Buna, the Japanese waged a prolonged stand in that area throughout December. MacArthur finally sent General Robert Eichelberger to command, ordering him to take Buna or 'don't come back alive'. Reinforced by a fresh Australian brigade, Eichelberger led his troops through the stinking malarial jungle and eliminated the last pocket of Japanese resistance on 21 January 1943. But the directive of 4 January from Imperial General Headquarters had ordered not only the abandonment of Guadalcanal but also of Papua, since control of the air and sea had passed to the Allies and it was no longer possible to supply and reinforce the Papuan operations.

The fighting in the Papuan campaign had consisted largely of savage hand to hand conflicts in the jungle and mountains. The Australians had borne the brunt of the campaign and showed it with 5700 battle casualties, while the Americans had 2800. But the Japanese forces had shown their true mettle and given the Allies an unpleasant taste of what was yet to come. Skilled in the arts of defensive warfare in difficult terrain, the Japanese soldiers were also possessed by a cult of death. All recruits to the Japanese Army received an intensive three-month indoctrination course to prepare them to die for their Emperor, their country and the honor of their regiment. Many officers and men in fact had their funeral rites performed before leaving for overseas service to signify their intention to die in action. The results spoke for

FOLLOWING PAGE: *The light cruiser* Biloxi *fires her 6-inch guns during a practice shoot.*

RIGHT: *Douglas C-47 Skytrains at Finschafen in north-east New Guinea in December 1943.*

BELOW: *A group of A6M3 Zeros at Rabaul in 1943. By the end of 1943 the once formidable Japanese base at Rabaul had been so heavily attacked by Allied air forces that it could be disregarded and bypassed.*

themselves – of 13,000 Japanese battle casualties in the Papuan campaign, only 38 were prisoners.

The second grand offensive had failed. It cost the Japanese dearly in irreplaceable resources. Their losses in ships and planes at Midway and through the Guadalcanal and Papua campaigns now precluded any effective offensive action, thus Japan would now be forced to fight a static defensive war. Although the strategic initiative lay with the enemy, the councils of the enemy were divided and a long lull in the action ensued.

MacArthur of the Army and Nimitz of the Navy were the two personalities who dominated not only the direction of operations but also the development of strategy in the Pacific. Early in the war, Roosevelt and Churchill had decided that the Pacific including Australia should be under the direction of the American Joint Chiefs of Staff. The Pacific area was further divided between MacArthur's Southwest Pacific Command, comprising Australia, New Guinea, the Philippines and most of the Netherlands East Indies, and the Central Pacific Command of Nimitz. Such a clumsy arrangement, dictated as it was by inter-service rivalry, not surprisingly produced two divergent strategies for the Pacific.

The naval chiefs adamantly advocated a purely naval campaign westward from Hawaii via the Gilbert, Marshall, Caroline and Mariana Islands to Japan. Such a campaign would enable them to use their large and growing force of aircraft carriers to better advantage than in the crowded waters around New Guinea and to fulfill their concept of using carrier task forces to isolate and dominate a group of islands. There would also be no question of flank attacks on the Southwest Pacific from the Micronesian 'spider webs' which the Japanese had spread across the Pacific, since these would become the main objects of attack. Another factor was simply that the Navy did not want naval forces under Army command, especially the potent new carriers with all their possibilities. The Navy felt MacArthur should stay on the defensive in the Southwest Pacific and let Nimitz get on with defeating Japan.

Such a role was unacceptable to MacArthur, who determined to launch his own campaign north from Australia to Japan via New Guinea and the Philippines. He wanted the entire Pacific fleet placed under his command to cover the advance along what he termed the 'New Guinea – Mindanao Axis'. The argument of the Navy was in fact strategically sound but MacArthur was taking other factors into consideration. The débâcle of the colonial powers had cost them great prestige in Asian eyes. As the United States

had been driven out of the Philippines by force of arms, MacArthur felt strongly that control of these islands had to be regained by the same means: otherwise the United States would never be able to reassert its prewar authority. In MacArthur's view, the only road to Tokyo which took account of American interests in Asia lay through the Philippine Islands.

Fond of this sort of confrontation, Roosevelt had approved the divided command in the Pacific in the hope that the inter-service rivalry would produce more rapid results. At the Trident Conference of May 1943 in Washington, the Combined Chiefs of Staff of the Allies had approved both strategies. Thus the Japanese were to face one thrust from MacArthur through New Guinea, while a second thrust was delivered by Nimitz across the Pacific. The theory was that the Japanese would not be able to concentrate their forces to block either thrust successfully because of the continual threat of the other one. The reality was that inter-service politics prevented the Americans from achieving a unified command in the Pacific. Two relatively independent campaigns, however, required much larger forces and thus more time for preparations. Hence the Japanese were given a respite by their enemy until June 1943 when the new Allied offensive was scheduled to begin.

However much Allied councils may have been divided over strategy, so were the Japanese divided along the same inter-service lines. The differences were in fact so deep that the Japanese also initiated no action during this period. Both the Army and Navy agreed that all territory then held should be defended but there the agreement ceased. Naval leaders gave top priority to holding the Bismarcks and the remainder of the Solomon Islands to protect their great naval base at Truk, 1000 miles to the north in the Carolines. Land operations in New Guinea were the aim of the Army which considered these necessary for the security of Army-held territory in the Philippines and the Netherlands East Indies. As the stronger service, the views of the Army prevailed. The line of defense was to run from Santa Isabel and New Georgia in the Solomons to Lae in New Guinea with the New Guinea area under Army command and the Solomons under Navy direction. Command was centered at Rabaul, from which the 17th Army in the Solomons and the 18th Army in New Guinea were controlled. The naval forces were light, consisting only of cruisers and destroyers, but capital ships were available from Truk. The Japanese forces were considerably inferior to those of the enemy as there were only 410 aircraft, 55,000 troops in

New Guinea and about 40,000 in the Bismarcks and Solomons. A blocking strategy was, however, thought to be feasible, as ten to fifteen divisions and perhaps 850 planes could augment the defenses within six months. With over 40 Japanese divisions inactive in China and Manchuria, it was not that the Imperial General Headquarters was deficient in manpower: the available manpower was maldistributed. With its defensive strategy now set, the Army and the Navy prepared for the next Allied offensive.

The immediate goal of the Allies was to break the barrier formed by the Bismarck Archipelago and capture the Japanese headquarters at Rabaul in New Britain. MacArthur was to have strategic control of the New Guinea – Solomons operations with Admiral Halsey in tactical command. Each with a well deserved reputation for confident and aggressive leadership, these two commanders complemented each other well. In the first phase of the campaign, Halsey was to seize the Russell Islands west of Guadalcanal as air and naval bases and then occupy the Trobriand Islands for the same purpose. The second phase envisaged MacArthur advancing along the north coast of New Guinea to take the Japanese positions around Lae, while Halsey took points on New Georgia and Bougainville to complete the conquest of the Solomons. The third phase was an attack by MacArthur on New Britain as preparation for the last phase – the direct attack on Rabaul. The entire campaign was conceived as alternating strokes to keep the Japanese off balance over a period of eight months. The 30th of June 1943 was D-Day.

The Allies had ample strength to achieve their objectives. Under MacArthur were four American and three Australian divisions, augmented by eight Australian divisions in training and the later arrival of two more American divisions. Over 1000 planes were also available. To these forces were added the 1800 planes and seven divisions under Halsey who also commanded six battleships and two carriers. Thus there was a comfortable margin of strength over the Japanese in all categories.

The landings in the Russells and Trobriands went uncontested while little initial resistance was encountered as the drive on Lae began. Soon, however, 6000 Japanese began to slow the Allied forces which did not reach Salamaua until mid-August. The attack by Halsey on New Georgia met immediate and heavy opposition as the 10,000-man garrison had been ordered by Imperial General Headquarters to hold as long as possible. Halsey had in fact received intelligence that Japanese reinforcements were land-

ing in southern New Georgia and advanced his landings in that area to 21 June but no Japanese were discovered. Overall, the Japanese resistance on New Georgia was serious enough that the inexperienced American troops made little progress despite overwhelming artillery, naval gun and air support. A further division and a half were thrown into the fray but even so, the remains of the Japanese garrison did not retreat to the neighboring island of Kolombangara until 5 August. Japanese casualties were about 2500 killed and 17 warships lost against 1000 Allied casualties and six warships.

But the New Georgia campaign brought about an important change in Allied tactics. MacArthur and Nimitz realized that 'island hopping' or methodically reducing each Japanese position in turn was not only costly and time-consuming but gave ample time to the enemy to strengthen the next position. Island hopping was an ineffective use of the air and naval superiority pos-

ABOVE: *Donald E. Runyon, a leading US Navy ace, in the cockpit of his Wildcat aboard the carrier* Enterprise *in August 1942.*

ABOVE RIGHT: *Curtiss Helldivers aboard the second carrier* Yorktown *in 1943.*

RIGHT: *A sailor at work on a 40mm AA gun aboard the* Missouri. *His tattoos commemorate former shipmates lost aboard the* Vincennes *in 1942.*

sessed by the Allies. 'Leap-frogging' was to be the new tactic, which meant by-passing the stronger Japanese positions, sealing them off by air and sea, and leaving them to 'wither on the vine', or as a baseball fan on MacArthur's staff described it, 'hittin' 'em where they ain't'. The first instance of leap-frogging was the by-passing of Kolombangara with its 10,000 defenders in favor of Vella Lavella with its 250-man garrison. The Japanese response in this case was to evacuate the garrison of Kolombangara to Bougainville as soon as the Allied tactic was evident. The development of leap-frogging as a tactic was to give new impetus to the lagging operations both in New Guinea and the Solomons.

MacArthur's drive on Lae was initially off-schedule, but a neat series of converging and flanking attacks forced the evacuation of Salamaua on 11 September and of Lae on 15 September 1943. Thus by mid-September the Allies were close to completion of the second phase of their offensive. All that remained was the capture of Bougainville by Halsey for the ring to begin closing around Rabaul.

September was a difficult month for the Imperial General Staff in Tokyo. In that month, not only did the failure of the blocking strategy have to be acknowledged but also the implications of the failure of Japan's whole policy towards the United States. Recovering from their initial defeat and demoralization in a remarkably short time, the Americans now held uncontested mastery of the sea and air. The imposing forces of MacArthur were steadily driving in the southwest flank while Nimitz was assembling the largest flotilla of ships since the Grand Fleet of Admiral Jellicoe in World War I for a mortal thrust across the Pacific. Clearly Imperial General Headquarters had been over optimistic in its assessment of its own defensive and American offensive capabilities. A careful estimate was therefore made of the minimum area needed for the maintenance of Japan's basic war aims. Termed the 'zone of absolute national defense', the area extended from Burma through Malaya and the Netherlands East Indies to west New Guinea and thence through the Carolines and Marianas to the Kuriles. All else – even the Bismarcks and Rabaul – was to be held for six months and then abandoned. Within these six months, it was planned to develop the zone of absolute national defense into a firm defense line, to treble Japanese aircraft production, and to build up the Combined Fleet to challenge once again the American Pacific Fleet in battle.

This plan was called the 'New Operational Policy' and only required that six Japanese divisions (none had ever been transferred from China and Manchuria) in the Southwest Pacific with little air and naval support, hold off 20-odd Allied divisions supported by 3000 aircraft. The element of unreality about the plan is accounted for by two factors. One is that Yamamoto, perhaps the only genius and surely the most realistic leader produced by Japan during the war, had died in the spring of 1943 when his plane was ambushed and shot down by American fighters. The other is that such was the secrecy maintained over the course of the war that even most of the Japanese military was unaware of the true situation and tended to be over-optimistic.

The real problem of Japan in 1943 was, however, of a much more fundamental nature. Having conquered a large empire with vast natural and economic resources, the Japanese had failed to organize their economy for all-out war production in the same manner as the United States and Britain. Planes and ships were needed to defend the far-flung maritime empire and yet by 1943, Japan was acutely short of both due to lack of planning. In 1943 alone, Japan produced only one-fifth as many planes as the United States and, equally important, had failed to undertake a program of training and mobilizing pilots. The quality of Japanese air pilots had dropped radically during 1942 and was an important factor in the rapid erosion of Japanese air strength. There were but three carriers under construction in Japan in 1943 as opposed to 22 in the United States. There had also been little provision made for building the merchant shipping necessary to hold a maritime empire together. American air and submarine attacks were taking a heavy toll, sinking over one million tons in 1942 alone. Much of the available merchant shipping had been squandered trying to support the wasteful operations in the Solomons which also had consumed over 3000 aircraft and their crews. Although Japan controlled the rich oil fields of the Netherlands East Indies, there was not enough shipping by 1943 to move the fuel. Thus an acute shortage of oil was curtailing operations of the Navy and grounding such aircraft as there were. The real weakness of Japan was organizational and economic.

MacArthur and Halsey were pushing their own operations at this point due to the impending start of the rival campaign in the central Pacific in November 1943. Halsey was under pressure as many of his ships had been on short loan from the Central Pacific Command and were now being recalled, as was the 2nd Marine Division. Similarly, MacArthur knew that priority was being given to the new offensive by

the Joint Chiefs of Staff who now considered that Rabaul should be by-passed. Halsey accordingly attacked Bougainville, the most westerly of the Solomons, in October 1943, thereby initiating another protracted struggle which lasted until March 1944. Manned by 40,000 soldiers and 20,000 sailors, the main defenses were in the south of this large island. To the surprise of the Japanese, the main American landings were shrewdly made on the weakly defended west coast. The Japanese made little response as over 60,000 Americans established a comfortable bridgehead over ten miles wide. The real contest began only at the end of February 1944 when the Japanese had finally traversed 50 miles of jungle. Hopelessly underestimating American strength at 20,000 combat troops, the Japanese commander attacked with 15,000 men in March. In a two-week struggle, 8000 Japanese died assaulting the well dug-in Americans who suffered only 300 losses. The remains of the shattered Japanese on Bougainville were then left to wither and die.

Pursuing his ultimate object of isolating Rabaul, MacArthur was fighting his way up the New Guinea coast. Using his favorite tactics of converging, pincer attacks and leap-frogging, MacArthur forced Imperial Headquarters to order a continuous series of withdrawals. By April 1944 the Japanese had been forced back to Wewak where the 18th Army dug in 50,000 troops in a strong position. The Joint Chiefs of Staff had already directed that Rabaul be

ABOVE: *This
Grumman Avenger
was said to be the first
US aircraft to land on
Peleliu after its
capture from the
Japanese in 1944.*

LEFT: *A Navy pilot
relives a successful
combat over Rabaul
on his return to his
base on Bougainville,
February 1944.*

isolated and left to wither, as it contained 100,000 defenders under a tough and resourceful leader with ample supplies stockpiled for previous expeditions which had come to nought. Even so, it was necessary to ensure that no flanking attack came from New Britain to menace the coastal drive in New Guinea, and MacArthur attacked Cape Gloucester across the straits from the New Guinea coast. The cape was held by 8000 Japanese troops recently arrived from China, but they were separated by 300 miles of rough terrain from any support from Rabaul. With little air support, their wisest course was to make the long retreat to Rabaul which they soon did. Several weeks of stiff resistance on the Admiralty Islands was overcome in early March, thus providing the Allies with another major air and naval base. This operation completed the breaking of the Bismarck Barrier and left Rabaul completely isolated.

The Japanese defense of New Guinea was now becoming chaotic and sporadic. The Central Pacific offensive meant that no support could be received from the Japanese forces in that sector. Troop convoys from China were suffering severe losses from attacks by American submarines while the forces already in New Guinea tended to be too dispersed for effective resistance. The 18th Army concentrated at Wewak was now by-passed by MacArthur who planned to arrive at the northwest point of New Guinea in four operations. Supported by Halsey's Seventh Fleet, MacArthur's army aboard a flotilla of 215 LSTs and LCTs successively conquered Wadke, Biak, Noemfoor and Sansapoor. Biak was a particularly tough fight as the Japanese had prepared a skilled defense in depth. But on 30 July 1944, the capture of Sansapoor completed Allied control of New Guinea and represented the last stop on that island on MacArthur's road back to the Philippines. There were still the remnants of five Japanese divisions in New Guinea, but Australian troops would welcome the opportunity to mop these up, leaving MacArthur to look across the Celebes Sea at Mindanao.

5.
Across the
Central Pacific

Although the offensive of his rival Mac-Arthur had begun in earnest in July 1942, Nimitz had been forced to wait until November 1943 before launching the Navy's cherished sweep across the Pacific. The offensive was not aimed at Japan itself but was intended to mop up the Japanese island fortresses and converge on the Philippines with that of MacArthur. With the American position in the Philippines restored, it was thought that American forces would establish large bases in China from which heavy bombers could hammer Japan into submission. The first attack in the Nimitz offensive was to be against the Gilbert Islands with Makin and Tarawa the main targets. Under the tactical command of Vice-Admiral Raymond Spruance, the victor of Midway, 7000 troops were to assault Makin while 18,000 attempted Tarawa. Over 1000 aircraft, six fleet carriers, five light carriers, and six new battleships were in support. A service fleet intended to supply and service the battle fleet made Spruance virtually independent in terms of logistics.

The assault began on 20 November against a force of 800 defenders on Makin and 3000 on Tarawa. The defense was not as strong as

ABOVE: *A view of Kwajalein after its capture. The damage done by the pre-landing bombardment is evident.*

RIGHT: *Admiral Marc Mitscher was one of the US Navy's top carrier admirals. He led the fleet carrier groups throughout 1944-45.*

BELOW: *The 5-inch secondary guns of the old battleship* New Mexico *fire on Guam, July 1944.*

planned because the reinforcements envisaged under the New Operational Policy had not yet arrived. An inexperienced Army division needed four days to overrun Makin, but the defenses of Tarawa proved a different matter. The three-day battle opened with a massive naval (3000 tons of shells in two and one half hours) and air bombardment, after which 5000 men of the 2nd Marine Division set out for the beaches in landing craft. One third had never reached the beach under the murderous Japanese fire but the remainder slowly forced the dogged Japanese back into two fortified points midway on the island. Surrounded, the defenders annihilated themselves in a series of suicidal counterattacks on the night of the 22nd. The costly assault on the Gilberts set off instant controversy in the United States but proved an invaluable testing ground and led to refinements in the assault techniques later used.

The next target was the Marshall Islands, but here Nimitz modified his strategy. Instead of striking at the easternmost islands, he chose to bypass them in favor of Kwajalein 400 miles beyond. Once Kwajalein was secured, Spruance was to be sent to seize Eniwetok at the far end of the chain. The arrangements were the same as the campaign in the Gilberts except that the pre-

paratory bombardment was to be four times as heavy. This new tactic of leap-frogging had an added benefit, as the Japanese reinforcements had been sent to the eastern Marshalls in anticipation of an attack in that quarter.

The fast carrier forces of Admiral Mark Mitscher neutralized any Japanese air and sea intervention and destroyed 150 enemy planes in the process as the main attack on Kwajalein opened on 1 February 1944. The 8000 defenders destroyed themselves by repeated 'banzai' charges which cost the Americans only 370 casualties, a far cry from the slaughter on Tarawa. Eniwetok subsequently succumbed after a three-day fight.

The Japanese found it impossible to react. The Combined Fleet, based at Truk, was merely a shadow of its former self, with the carriers still in Japan training replacement air groups and the cruiser force, attacked by the Americans at Rabaul, virtually a nonentity. It became even less effective in mid-February when Task Force 58 attacked Truk itself, forcing a withdrawal to Palau. As this threatened the flank of Mac-Arthur's advance in New Guinea, however,

Palau was also attacked in late March and Combined Fleet Headquarters under Admiral Koga Mineichi, who had replaced Yamamoto when the latter was killed in June 1943, was removed to Mindanao. Unfortunately Koga was killed in the process when his seaplane crashed in bad weather, and he was replaced by Admiral Toyoda Soemu who decided to set up his headquarters in Japan, delegating the sea-going command known as the First Mobile Fleet, to Vice-Admiral Ozawa Jisaburo. It was to be a fatal split, denying initiative to the commander on the spot and subjecting the Japanese navy to the false hopes and political machinations of Tokyo.

The results were apparent in the intricate plan put forward by Toyoda (Operation A-Go), designed to bring about 'a decisive battle with full strength . . . at a favorable opportunity.' The idea was to lure the American fleet into one of two battle areas (the Palau or the Caroline Islands), chosen because they were within range of the myriad of island air bases from which Japanese air strength could participate to help balance the American carriers. A portion of the Japanese fleet was to be used as bait, sailing openly into the

ABOVE: *The low seawall at Tarawa provided virtually the only shelter from Japanese fire for the attacking Marines.*

ABOVE RIGHT: *Casualties on the beach at Tarawa. A lack of information on tides and topography was often a problem during landings on isolated Pacific locations. At Tarawa many Marines had to attempt to wade ashore long distances under Japanese fire because of this.*

RIGHT: *A Sherman tank on Kwajalein.*

chosen area, and as soon as the Americans re-acted the main portion under Ozawa was to leave its anchorage at Tawi Tawi in the Sulu Archipe-lago, proceed to an area east of the Philippines and take the enemy by surprise. It was an opti-mistic scenario, but once the Americans threatened the Mariana Islands, the next logical step after the Marshalls, the Japanese had to do something. The Marianas, consisting principally of the islands of Guam, Saipan and Tinian, were part of the inner defense line round Japan itself and represented an ideal base for American stra-tegic bombers. By May 1944 Toyoda had dis-patched the carriers to join Ozawa, despite their lack of trained air groups, and had concentrated a total of 1700 aircraft at shore bases in the Dutch East Indies, the Philippines, New Guinea and the Bismarcks. As American intentions be-came clear, more than 500 of these machines were moved forward into the Marianas.

This was the first Japanese mistake, for while Vice-Admiral Richmond Turner's Amphibious Force prepared for the assault on Saipan, set for 15 June, the carriers of Task Force 58 roamed far and wide, hitting Japanese bases. After neu-

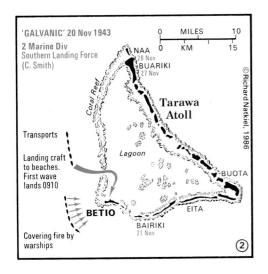

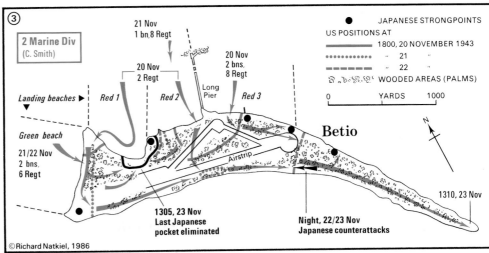

ABOVE: *The landings on Tarawa. In proportion to the size of the force employed, casualties in this operation were the worst in US military history.*

ABOVE LEFT: *A cruiser moves up to its bombardment position off Orote Point, Guam, passing a group of transport ships.*

BELOW LEFT: *The battleship USS* Pennsylvania *in dock for repairs later in the war.*

tralizing strikes against Palau, Yap and Woleai in late March, they moved southward to support MacArthur in Hollandia and on their return to the Central Pacific in May, pounded Truk, Marcus and Wake Islands. At the same time, shore-based bombers hit the by-passed Marshall Islands of Jaluit and Wotje. Japanese aircraft and installations were destroyed in each attack, gradually undermining Toyoda's plan. The process reached a climax on 11, 12 and 13 June as Mitscher's force moved in to soften up the Marianas and interdict Japanese supply routes through the islands of Chichi Jima and Iwo Jima, 650 miles to the north. By the time the Marines invaded Saipan, the 500 aircraft in the Marianas had largely been eliminated, complete American air superiority had been achieved and one of the main elements of Operation A-Go had effectively been destroyed.

Neither Toyoda nor Ozawa was aware of the true state of air losses (the local commander neglected to tell them for fear of repercussions), and when the decision to seek battle was taken on 13 June, both retained a degree of optimism about its outcome. Practical problems continued to emerge, forcing changes to the original plan. In late May the defenders of the island of Biak, an important air base in the efforts to halt MacArthur's advance, had called urgently for aid, and a special naval force under Vice-Admiral Ugaki Matome, composed of the battleships *Yamato* and *Musashi* with cruisers and destroyers had been detached from Ozawa's command. This had now to be recalled and directed to rendezvous with the rest of the fleet in the Philippine Sea, a maneuver which was to take time and preclude the original scheme whereby it was 'to lure the enemy fleet.' The two forces met on 16 June, but surprise was quickly lost. American submarines saw and reported both portions, allowing Vice-Admiral Raymond

Spruance time to assess the danger and make the necessary dispositions. The last great carrier battle was about to begin.

On the American side, Spruance realized that the Japanese could not approach to within range until 19 June, and he was not prepared to advance far into the Philippine Sea to meet them. His first duty was the protection of Turner's Amphibious Force, so he ordered his carriers to complete their neutralization of Japanese bases on Guam, Tinian, Chichi Jima and Iwo Jima before rendezvousing 180 miles west of the Marianas on 18 June. Once assembled, Task Force 58 was formidable. Its 15 carriers were divided into four self-contained task groups (TG 58-1 comprising *Hornet*, *Yorktown*, *Belleau Wood* and *Bataan*; TG 58-2 *Bunker Hill*, *Wasp*, *Monterey* and *Cabot*; TG 58-3 *Enterprise*, *Lexington*, *Princeton* and *San Jacinto*; TG 58-4 *Essex*, *Langley* and *Cowpens*), each with its complement of battleships, cruisers and destroyers. The total strength exceeded 900 aircraft. In normal circumstances the task groups would have fought as separate entities, but with the prospect of a major fleet action, Spruance altered their organization. The battleships of the carrier group escorts were formed into a 'Battle Line' (known as TG 58-7) under Vice-Admiral Willis Lee with four heavy cruisers and 13 destroyers transferred from Turner's Amphibious Force as an escort. This was pushed forward 15 miles ahead of the carriers to act as a shield, with TG 58-4 in attendance to give air cover, while the other three carrier groups were stationed in a north-south line some 15 miles apart. It was basically a defensive formation, designed to trap and destroy incoming Japanese air or surface assaults.

Meanwhile Ozawa's force continued to approach the Marianas from the west. It was organized into three parts. A Force, under Ozawa himself, was centered upon the three big

fleet carriers *Taiho*, *Zuikaku* and *Shokaku*, with a screen of cruisers and destroyers and provided the main air strength with 207 aircraft. B Force, commanded by Rear Admiral Joshima, contained the slower fleet carriers *Junyo* and *Hiyo* as well as the light carrier *Ryuho*, which between them mustered 135 aircraft. It was protected by one battleship, one cruiser and nine destroyers. These two groups operated independently about 12 miles apart, while C or Van Force under Vice-Admiral Kurita comprised the four battleships *Yamato*, *Musashi*, *Haruna* and *Kongo*, four heavy cruisers, a light cruiser and nine destroyers screening three light carriers *Chitose*, *Chiyoda*, and *Zuiho* with a combined complement of 90 aircraft. These sailed about 100 miles in advance to draw the fire of enemy air strikes and extend the range of reconnaissance seaplanes.

In fact it was in the area of reconnaissance that the Japanese enjoyed about their only advantage, for their float planes, catapulted from battleships and cruisers, had a greater endurance than their American counterparts. Because of this Ozawa was aware of Spruance's dispositions on 18 June and in a position to plan a strike, at a range of approximately 350 miles, for dawn the next day. Spruance, on the other hand, with reconnais-

sance aircraft that reached the limit of their fuel about 60 miles short of the Japanese fleet, spent 18 June in ignorance of enemy movements, his latest reports having come in 24 hours earlier from the submarine *Cavalla*, shadowing A Force. It was not until 1000 hours on 19 June, when the radar of Lee's Battle Line detected a swarm of incoming aircraft, that the Americans were able to react. Even so, they managed to inflict the first casualties, for as Ozawa's A Force launched its strike aircraft, the submarine *Albacore* attacked and damaged the carrier *Taiho*. It was but a foretaste of things to come.

As soon as the Japanese air armada, divided into three waves and comprising nearly 250 assorted dive bombers, torpedo bombers and fighters, was detected, the American carriers turned together into the wind, launched any bombers or torpedo aircraft on deck, sending them out of the way to the eastward, and concentrated solely upon fighters. Nearly 300 Hellcats took to the air, some of them flying over Guam to attack the few shore-based aircraft which the Japanese brought into the battle, but the vast majority advancing to intercept Ozawa's carrier strikes. The interceptions, which continued throughout the morning, usually took

ABOVE: *A Vought F4 Corsair flown by Lt Ira Kepford, an ace with 16 Japanese aircraft in his record when this photo was taken in May 1944.*

RIGHT: *A Dauntless is waved off from its carrier for an attack on Wake Island.*

RIGHT: *A Marine Corsair bombed up for an attack mission at an airfield in the Gilbert Islands.*

place some 45 to 60 miles in front of the American fleet and were so successful that they soon became known as 'The Great Marianas Turkey Shoot.' In the first Japanese wave, from C Force, out of 69 aircraft 42 were destroyed and none penetrated to the American ships. Of the second wave, comprising 128 planes from A Force, more than 100 were intercepted and shot down. The remainder broke through only to face the massed gunfire of the Battle Line, and an even smaller remnant managed to reach the aircraft carriers beyond. Minor damage was inflicted upon the *Wasp* and *Bunker Hill* of TG 58-2, but by 1200 hours it was all over. Less than 30 survivors limped back to the Japanese fleet with dangerously exaggerated tales of American carriers on fire and sinking. Meanwhile, the third wave, comprising 47 aircraft from B Force, had flown too far to the north. Just over half of them failed to make any contact with the Americans, returning to their carriers unmol-

ested, but the others succeeded in locating the most northerly task group, where they were pounced on by patrolling Hellcats. Seven of the Japanese aircraft were destroyed: the rest dumped their bombs ineffectively and fled. The Americans let them go.

But if Spruance was unable to hit the source of the Japanese air strikes, the same was not the case with his submarines, and as the morning came to an end a double disaster was inflicted by them upon Ozawa. At 1220 hours the *Cavalla*, after having lost contact with A Force during 18 June, suddenly found herself in an ideal position to attack the *Shokaku*. Three torpedoes tore into her side, starting fires which the crew tried desperately to fight for nearly three hours. But their efforts were in vain: at the end of that time gasoline vapor exploded and the *Shokaku*, one of the last remaining elements of Nagumo's Pearl Harbor force, went to the bottom. At almost the same time the *Taiho*, apparently little damaged

ABOVE: *Pilots of VF-16 are briefed by their squadron commander aboard the carrier* Lexington *during the operations in the Gilbert Islands in November 1943.*

by *Albacore*'s earlier attack, also exploded when fumes from a ruptured fuel system ignited. Ozawa's best ships had gone down.

In the meantime, further Japanese air strikes, launched from the *Zuikaku* of A Force and the three light carriers of B Force, tried to break through to the American ships. Of the planes involved, only about half located the southern carrier task group and were promptly hit by waiting Hellcats. Few of the Japanese machines survived. The remainder, 49 strong, headed for Guam to refuel before restarting their search. But they were unaware of the true state of affairs on the island, dominated by the Americans since dawn. Set upon by 27 Hellcats, 30 Japanese planes were shot down over the sea or as they tried to land on the battered airstrip. By 1600 hours the Americans had cleared the air entirely of enemy machines and, except for action against the occasional shore-based raider, no more air fighting took place on 19 June. Japan's naval air arm had been all but destroyed. Of the 373 aircraft sent out from Ozawa's carriers, only 130 had returned; a figure which dropped to 102 as pilot inexperience showed itself in a series of crashes as the survivors relanded. In addition, about 50 land-based aircraft had been destroyed. Such losses were irreplaceable: Japan would be unable to man or equip an effective carrier force again. American losses, by way of comparison, had been only 29 aircraft. Spruance's defensive stance had been justified.

But the Battle of the Philippine Sea was not over, for the Americans, brought up to believe that no naval action could be termed a success

ABOVE: *The batman guides an aircraft in to land on the carrier* Wasp.

RIGHT: *Deck activities aboard the carrier* Cowpens *during the Gilbert Islands operations. As can be seen the personnel are wearing clothing of different colors. This was a deliberate policy so that men with different duties could easily be distinguished and their work co-ordinated.*

LEFT: *Marines turn a captured Japanese gun on its former owners during the fighting on Saipan, June 1944.*

RIGHT: *Admiral Spruance (left) and General Holland Smith during the Saipan invasion.*

BELOW: *Marines under fire on the beach at Saipan. In the background is a Buffalo amphibious tractor equipped with a gun turret for close support.*

without the destruction of the enemy fleet, were determined to go over to the offensive. This was not possible immediately, however, as Spruance was still not aware of Ozawa's position. In fact the American Task Force had drifted eastward during the air battle, increasing the distance between the two fleets to something like 400 miles, outside the range of Mitscher's strike aircraft. Therefore, as a first move, Task Force 58 had to turn westward to try and close the gap while sending out reconnaissance missions in all directions. No sign of the Japanese was reported during the remainder of 19 June, and it began to look as if Ozawa had escaped.

If the Japanese commander had realized the full state of his losses there is little doubt that he would have withdrawn swiftly, but Ozawa was unaware of the extent of his defeat. Not only did he believe the stories brought back to him about American aircraft and carriers destroyed, but he was also convinced that many of his missing strike planes had landed on Guam or neighboring islands and were ready to take to the air again. As a result, on 20 June, having withdrawn northwestward to rendezvous with replenishment tankers he was prepared to renew the battle at the earliest opportunity. It was only when his communications staff intercepted a signal from an American aircraft at 1615 hours on 20 June, reporting contact with the Japanese fleet that worries began to arise. Refueling was postponed and Ozawa retired further northwestward, hoping to outpace the Americans before nightfall and so avoid an air strike which, with only 100 aircraft left, he would be unable to counter.

He very nearly succeeded. When the Americans received the long-awaited signal of contact at about 1600 hours, the chances of putting in a successful strike were slim. The enemy fleet was only just within range and, even if aircraft were launched immediately they would have to be relanded after dark, a procedure for

which the American pilots were not trained. But Spruance and Mitscher were not going to let the opportunity slip by, and within half an hour of the reported sighting 77 Dauntless dive bombers, 54 Avenger torpedo bombers and 85 Hellcat fighters had taken to the air, heading west into the setting sun. Their mission was a resounding success. After a section broke away to deal with Ozawa's refueling force of six tankers, the remainder swept aside the thin screen of Zero fighter protection and pounded the Japanese fleet, concentrating upon the carriers. After 20 minutes of frenetic action the *Hiyo* had been torpedoed and sunk, the *Zuikaku* crippled, the *Chiyoda* set on fire, the battleship *Haruna* and the cruiser *Maya* damaged. In addition, a further 65 planes of the Japanese naval air arm had been destroyed, leaving Ozawa with less than 40 operational machines. Admitting defeat at last, he fled to Okinawa. American losses were slight, for although nearly 80 of the returning aircraft crashed as they tried to reland after nightfall, few

crew members were killed. Indeed, after widespread rescue operations only 16 pilots and 33 aircrew were reported missing. The Battle of the Philippine Sea – an American victory of epic proportions – was over. The Japanese naval air arm had been destroyed and her carriers were reduced to impotence, denied the ability either to strike or to defend themselves in future.

The land fighting on the Mariana Islands had already begun before the fleets engaged in their unequal struggle. The air attacks on the islands have already been noted and were augmented by heavy gun bombardments from 11 June. A total of some 127,000 troops arrived off Saipan in the ships of the Fifth Fleet and landings began on 15 June. Following a feint attack by reserve regiments, the main attack was made in two separate thrusts, each by a Marine division, on each side of Afetna Point. Although there were about 30,000 Japanese on Saipan instead of the 20,000 anticipated, the Americans crossed the island within three days, splitting the Japanese forces into two parts.

The southern part was easily dealt with by a single infantry battalion, and the remaining infantry joined the Marines in the drive against the northern defenders. In this, the infantry moved slower than the Marines, which spared them the high casualty rate suffered by the latter but aroused some ill-feeling on the part of the Marine commanders. As the Japanese were pushed up into the narrower part of the island their position became hopeless. A final suicidal counterattack was pushed back by the US infantry and resistance more or less ceased, with 2000 Japanese consenting to be captured. American dead, at a little more than 3000, were only one ninth of the Japanese killed.

After Saipan came Guam, where the Japanese had 13,000 soldiers and over 5000 sailors. American landing tactics again involved the separate landing of two Marine divisions, one on each side of a coastal objective, this time the Orote Peninsula. The two divisions, after some fighting, managed to link up to create a wide bridgehead before turning northward against the

ABOVE: *An F6 Hellcat makes a hard landing aboard the carrier* Cowpens.

main Japanese strength. The Japanese retreated only slowly, launching determined counterattacks at every opportunity, and held out until they were pushed to the very tip of the island at Mount Machanao. Again, the Japanese dead at 17,300 were about nine times the American loss. Some of the Japanese, rejecting both suicide and capture, hid in the jungle and reappeared after the war was over, in one case 27 years after the Japanese surrender.

While the struggle for Guam was in progress, other landings were made on Tinian. Here the tactics of the two Marine divisions were different. One was used to make a feint attack while the other landed on two beaches in the northern extremity of the island, where it was joined by the division that had made the feint. The Japanese had only about 9000 men on the island, and their night counterattack on the beachheads was weak. The Marines then pushed south until the defenders were crammed into the southern end of the island, where resistance ceased at the beginning of August. This time the Japanese killed, at 6000, were 20 times more numerous than the American dead. The road to the Philippines was now open.

The fall of Saipan was such a disaster for Japan that it could not be hidden in the same manner as earlier disasters like Midway. The disquiet was so intense that the government of Tojo Hideki fell, to be replaced by that of General Koiso Kuniacki. Despite its desperate situation, the Japanese military still hoped to fight the war to a drawn peace and thus maintained their warlike posture while secretly trying to open negotiations with the United States.

BELOW: *An Army Air Force Liberator bomber in flight over Makin shortly after its capture late in 1943.*

6.
Return to the Philippines

By the end of July 1944, General Mac-Arthur's Southwest Pacific Command had gained control of New Guinea and was poised to cross the Celebes Sea to Mindanao, but the argument on future strategy was still fiercely contested. Admiral Ernest J. King and most other Navy planners in Washington wanted to bypass the Philippines in favour of an attack on Formosa or even the Home Islands themselves. MacArthur waxed eloquent on the need to recapture the major part of the Philippines – partly for strategic reasons, but primarily because he had given his word to return. Failure to do so, he maintained, would compromise American honor and prestige in the Far East for many years to come. Admiral Nimitz was in the middle. He took a dim view of skipping over the Philippines altogether, but was willing to con-

sider bypassing Luzon if major air and naval bases could be established in the central and southern Philippines.

The stalemate seemed unresolvable when President Roosevelt intervened and decided to have a meeting with Nimitz and MacArthur at Pearl Harbor to discuss the next moves. During the meeting on 26 and 27 July, MacArthur and Nimitz talked while the President and the others listened. In the end, all were convinced of the merits of MacArthur's 'Leyte then Luzon' concept. In September the Allied Combined Chiefs of Staff, meeting at the Octagon Conference in Quebec, agreed that MacArthur and Nimitz should converge on Leyte in December, but within a week Admiral Halsey, who had sent out task forces of his Third Fleet headed by the new *Essex* class fast carriers to soften up Morotai,

RIGHT: *The landings on Leyte which began the campaign to recapture the Philippines.*

FAR RIGHT: *General Douglas MacArthur in a typical proud and confident pose.*

BELOW: *The US escort carriers come under Japanese shell fire during the critical stages of the Battle of Leyte Gulf, a photo taken from the* White Plains.

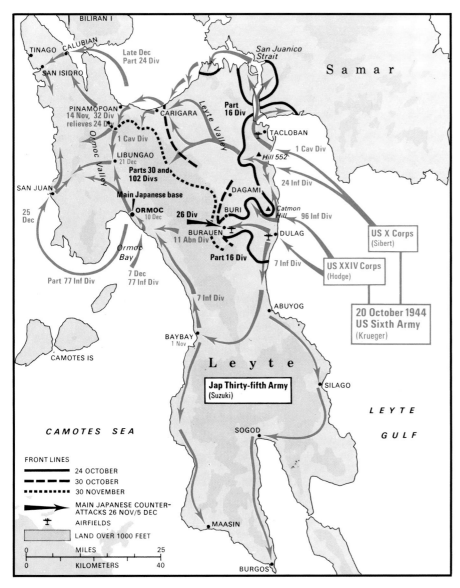

Yap, and the Palau Islands, reported meeting few Japanese planes and no warships. His story of the 'amazing and fantastic' lack of Japanese resistance put a different light on the matter. Without opposition, MacArthur's forces could make one long hop from New Guinea to Leyte, by-passing Mindanao completely. In an unusual example of strategic flexibility the Octagon Conference moved the date of the Leyte Mission up to 20 October.

By this time the Japanese were in grave difficulty, despite their many advantages, largely because Imperial General Headquarters had been operating with an outdated concept of war. They did not give naval airpower – the weapon upon which their defense should have relied – top priority. During 1943 America built 22 aircraft carriers; Japan produced only three and never managed to recruit enough pilots to man even a restricted air arm. Japan controlled 80 percent of the world's rubber along with vast quantities of oil, tin, tungsten, manganese, and iron ore – but had no way to exploit those re-

sources. A large merchant fleet was needed, but battleships had been given priority over an expanded merchant navy. By 1943 Japan was already facing a severe oil shortage and curtailed naval operations because it no longer had tanker capacity to transport the oil from the Netherlands East Indies. As a result of this basic economic weakness in their defense structure, the Japanese had been grimly hanging on since their defeat in Guadalcanal and Papua. Instead of fighting to win, they were now simply trying to hold on as long as possible.

Of all the services the newest, the naval air arm, suffered most. Between 1942 and 1944 Japan lost 8000 navy planes and enormous numbers of pilots. The planes could be replaced, albeit with difficulty, but the men could not. Casualties increased as the quality of new recruits and training procedures fell. With the death of Admiral Yamamoto, the major supporter of naval air power was gone and the navy soon returned to its first love, the battleship.

By March 1944 Japanese strategists could foresee the American invasion of the Philippines, long before Allied planners had managed to agree on it themselves. Japan was most concerned with holding Luzon, thus maintaining communication with Malaya and Indonesia. But she had to be prepared to defend not only all the Philippine Islands, but Formosa and the Ryukyus as well; if the inner defense line that extended from the Kuriles through the Home Islands to the Philippines was breached, Japan

ABOVE: *The destroyer* Heerman *laying smoke near the escort carrier* Kalinin Bay *during the action off Samar. The destroyers bravely screened the escort carriers from the Japanese.*

RIGHT: *The destroyer* Cony *lays smoke to shield the battleship* West Virginia *from Japanese air attack during the landings on Leyte.*

would lose her lines of communication through the Formosa Straits and the South China Sea and all the resources of the southern colonies, and would be forced to fall back on the resources of China alone. In July/August 1944, then, Japanese planners drew up four separate *Sho* (or victory) plans. *Sho-1* covered the Philippines while the others concerned Formosa-Ryukyus, Honshu-Kyushu, and Hokkaido-Kuriles. *Sho-1* was a typically Japanese plan that employed divided forces, diversions, unexpected attacks, and an elaborate time schedule. First the Northern Force under Admiral Ozawa, built around the four carriers *Zuikaku, Zuiho, Chitose,* and *Chiyoda,* would lure the main American force – Halsey's Third Fleet – to the north, away from the real objective. Then the Center Force commanded by Admiral Kurita, consisting of the giant battleships *Yamato* and *Musashi,* nine cruisers, and a destroyer screen, would come south of Luzon through the San Bernardino Strait into Leyte Gulf. At the same time Admiral Nishimura's Southern Force would move up on the gulf through the Surigao Strait between Leyte and Mindanao. The two forces would converge, destroy shipping in the gulf, smash the Allied bridgehead, and presumably depart before the Third Fleet could return. The carriers were being used as decoys because the naval air force had already been virtually eliminated – there were only 116 planes on Ozawa's four carriers, and less than 200 in land-based air groups in the Ryukyus, Formosa, and Manila. If the plan succeeded the American army at Leyte

would be destroyed as completely as the navy had been three years earlier at Pearl Harbor, and Japan would have gained at least a year's breathing space.

Ideally, *Sho-1* would be timed to catch the Leyte landings in their 'naked' stage, as troops and equipment were being landed. But Japan's oil shortage was so great that if *Sho-1* was activated too soon, the ships would be short of fuel for the real engagement. Japanese intelligence had predicted a landing at Leyte during the last ten days of October, but could be certain of neither the time nor the place. Thus the Commander in Chief of the Combined Fleet, Admiral Toyoda Soemu, had to wait until American ships were actually seen entering Leyte Gulf before activating the plan. He was taking a last desperate gamble – that his forces, free from air attack, could make contact with the enemy and destroy them with overwhelming gun power. The Combined Fleet would probably be destroyed. But if the Philippines were lost, and Japan cut off from her only supply of oil, the fleet would be immobilized anyway.

Allied preparations for the Leyte landing began in September, immediately after the schedule was advanced by the Octagon Conference. Morotai was taken, to become a staging base for short-range fighters and light and medium bombers. Early in October, MacArthur's forces and those of the US Seventh Fleet under Admiral Thomas Kinkaid began to gather along the shores of New Guinea. The invasion group, when finally assembled, would contain 738 ships including 157 combat vessels, 420 amphibians, 73 service ships, and 84 patrol boats, as well as mine sweeping and hydrographic specialist craft. Supporting the convoy was Halsey's Third Fleet – 17 carriers, six battleships, 17 cruisers, and 64 destroyers. Altogether it was the most powerful naval force ever assembled (though not as large as the force that would attack Okinawa the following April). On 10 October the mine sweepers began to lead the enormous convoy away from the New Guinea coast, toward Leyte.

Between 12-14 October a major air attack was launched against Formosa: although Japan's weakness in the air had made the giant hop from New Guinea to Leyte possible, it was still necessary to destroy what remained of her land-based air power. Vice-Admiral Marc Mitscher, Commander of Task Force 38 which was part of the Third Fleet, sent a host of planes from his nine carriers against the island. More than 200 Japanese fighters rose to meet them but, as their commander Admiral Fukudome later lamented, they were 'nothing but so many eggs thrown against the wall. . . .' More than one third were lost on 12 October alone. Overall, Task Force 38 destroyed more than 500 Japanese planes and 40 transports and other vessels. A series of raids by China-based B-29s wreaked even more havoc on the island. During the next week Japanese air bases in Luzon, Mindanao, and the Netherlands East Indies were attacked from the air, and a naval force was sent against the Kurile Islands. There was little resistance from the Japanese, who were hoarding their planes for the 'general decisive battle' ahead.

For once the Allies had no advance knowledge of Japanese plans. MacArthur's staff discounted the idea that Japan might oppose the landings. General George Kenney, Commander of the Far East Army Air Forces considered that Leyte would be 'relatively undefended,' and on 20 October MacArthur's headquarters announced that the Japanese Navy would not use the San Bernardino or Surigao Straits because of navigational hazards and lack of space to maneuver. Admiral Halsey hoped very much that the Japanese fleet would come out and fight, but was not at all certain it would.

Events during the main landings did not dispel this view. The minesweepers had reached the entrances of Leyte Gulf on 17 October. By midday on 18 October the four islands (Dinagat, Calicoan, Suluan, and Homonhon) that mark the entrance to Leyte Gulf from the Philippine Sea had been taken by the 6th Ranger Infantry Battalion under Lieutenant Colonel H A Mucci. Rear Admiral Jesse Oldendorf had moved his fire support ships into the gulf and was bombarding the southern landing beaches to cover the underwater demolition teams. Bombardments continued through the next day, while planes from three groups of escort carriers (usually known as Taffy 1, Taffy 2, and Taffy 3) commanded by Rear Admiral Thomas Sprague attacked Japanese airfields and defenses on Leyte, Mindanao, and in the Visayans.

A-Day, 20 October, dawned with perfect weather and light surf. The fire support ships began their preliminary bombardment at 0700 hours and the troops began landing on schedule

BELOW: *General MacArthur watches the bombardment of Los Negros Island from the bridge of the* Phoenix, *February 1944.*

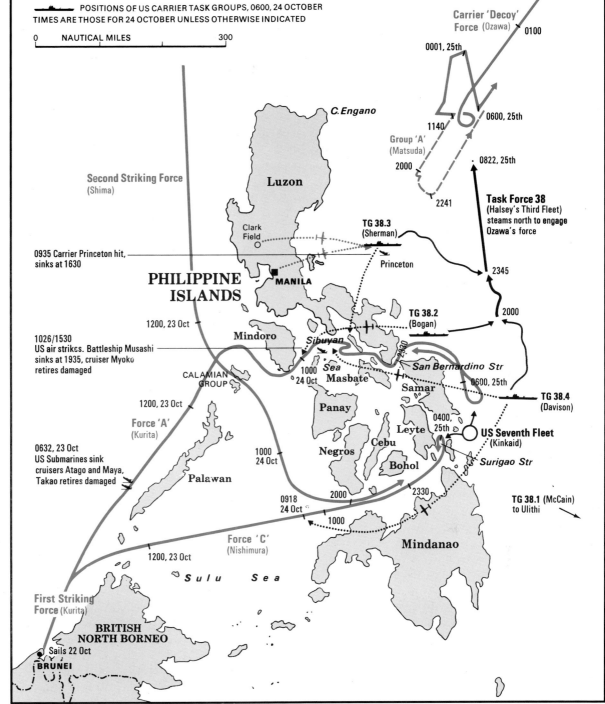

at 1000 hours, meeting only light mortar fire. After the first wave had landed, the moment for which MacArthur had been waiting for two and a half years arrived. Accompanied by Sergio Osmena, who had become President of the Philippines following the death of Manuel Quezon, the general embarked in a landing craft, got out into the water, and strode ashore. Standing on the beach, in a downpour of rain, he broadcast a message to the Philippine people: 'People of the Philippines, I have returned. By the grace of Almighty God, our forces stand again on Philippine soil – soil consecrated by the blood of our two peoples.' He urged the Filipinos to 'rally to

me . . . In the name of your sacred dead, strike! Let no heart be faint. Let every arm be steeled.' His words have since been alleged to have had an overwhelming impact in the Philippines and he urged Roosevelt, in a note dramatically scribbled out on the beach, to grant the Philippines independence immediately after the successful liberation campaign.

By midnight on 21 October, 132,000 men and 200,000 tons of equipment had been landed on Leyte; the airfields at Dulag and Tacloban, as well as the docking facilities in Tacloban town, were in American hands. By 22 October the assault landing portion of the operation was over.

Of the hundreds of ships that had jammed the Leyte Gulf, only 28 Liberty Ships and 25 Landing Ships, Medium (LSMs) and Landing Ships, Tank (LSTs) remained. On land, General Walter Krueger and the Sixth Army remained to root out the 60,000 Japanese who were still fiercely defending the island.

All this time there had been no sign of the Japanese fleet, and it looked as if the predictions of a virtually uncontested operation had come true. But in fact, Toyoda had only been informed on 17 October that the Allies were approaching Leyte Gulf, and had activated *Sho-1*. The next day Kurita's main battle force left Lingga Roads. On 20 October, after stopping for fuel at Brunei Bay in North Borneo, the force split. Kurita, with five battleships and most of the heavy cruisers, headed for the Sibuyan Sea and the San Bernar-

dino Straight. Nishimura's Southern Force crossed the Sulu Sea heading toward the Surigao Strait, supported by two heavy cruisers, a light cruiser, and seven destroyers – all under the command of Admiral Shima. Meanwhile, Ozawa and the Northern Carrier Force had begun their decoy mission.

At 0116 hours on 23 October two American submarines, *Darter* and *Dace*, who were patrolling the Palawan Passage between Palawan Island and the South China Sea, made radar contact with Kurita's Center Force. They sent off a report to Halsey, who received it gladly at 0620 hours; it was the first news he had of Center Force since it left Lingga. Twelve minutes later, *Darter* emptied her bow torpedo tubes at the heavy cruiser *Atago*, Kurita's flagship, which sank almost immediately. The two submarines

ABOVE: *PT Boats like PT-131 (shown) played an important part in the action in Surigao Strait which was one phase of the Battle of Leyte Gulf.*

RIGHT: *A Liberator bomber attacks Japanese positions on Corregidor Island in Manila Bay, one of the last Japanese positions in the Philippines to be taken.*

managed to sink another heavy cruiser and put a third out of commission before the day had ended. Early the next morning, however, *Darter* ran hard aground in the difficult channel and had to be abandoned. Kurita, who had swum over and raised his flag in the giant battleship *Yamato*, took Center Force on into the Sibuyan Sea.

The submarine's timely warning had enabled Halsey to prepare a warm reception for Kurita, and by noon on 24 October he had deployed three of Task Force 38's fast carrier groups on a broad front: Rear Admiral Sherman's group in the north, Rear Admiral Bogan's off the San Bernardino Strait, and Rear Admiral Davison's off Samar. Sherman was in the best position to damage Kurita, but before any of the groups could launch a strike, three waves of 50 to 60 Japanese planes each flew in from Luzon armed with bombs and torpedoes. Although many were shot down, one dive bomber broke through the anti-aircraft fire, escaped the Combat Air Patrol, and hit the light carrier *Princeton* which sank later that day.

Bogan and Davison were able to launch attacks, and since most of the Japanese planes were busy attacking Sherman, the Americans were able to hit Center Force hard. The great *Musashi* sustained hits from 19 torpedoes and 17 bombs, and sank with most of her crew.

At 1400 hours, Kurita, his repeated requests for air cover denied, pulled the Japanese ships west to regroup and assess damages; with four battleships, six heavy cruisers, two light cruisers, and ten destroyers left, Center Force was still a formidable fleet. Kurita asked permission to wait until nightfall before running the San Bernardino Strait, but Toyoda ordered him straight ahead. The Battle of the Sibuyan Sea

had put him seven hours behind schedule and there was already no way he could keep his dawn rendezvous in Leyte Gulf with Nishimura and the Southern Force.

Meanwhile, while Kurita was fighting in the Sibuyan Sea, Southern Force was making its own way toward Leyte Gulf. Nishimura's squadron – the battleships *Fuso* and *Yamashiro*, the heavy cruiser *Mogami*, and four destroyers – was in the lead, with Shima's supporting force several hours behind. They were first sighted by planes from the carriers *Enterprise* and *Franklin* at 0905 hours on 24 October. Admiral Kinkaid of the Seventh Fleet correctly estimated that the Japanese force intended to break into the Gulf via the Surigao Strait that night, and shortly after noon had alerted every ship under his command to prepare for the attack. At 1830 hours Nishimura knew that Kurita would not be able to rendezvous as scheduled; nevertheless, when he received a message from Toyoda about an hour later directing that 'all forces will dash to the attack, trusting in divine guidance,' he pushed on toward the strait without even waiting for Shima to catch up. Without air cover, the only chance he believed he had lay in getting into the Gulf under cover of darkness.

But Kinkaid and Rear Admiral Oldendorf, who commanded the Bombardment and Fire Support Group from the heavy cruiser *Louisville*, had laid a neat trap for anyone who tried to enter the gulf that night. Six battleships, four heavy cruisers, and four light cruisers were deployed along a 15-mile battle line between Leyte and Hibusan Island, where the Surigao Strait enters Leyte Gulf. Two destroyer divisions were sent down the strait to launch torpedo attacks, a third was in readiness as a follow-up, and a fourth attended the battle line. Since there were no radar-equipped aircraft available for night reconnaissance, 39 torpedo boats patrolled the strait, with orders to report any contact with the enemy and then attack.

The first contact was reported at 2230 hours, but none of the subsequent PT boat attacks managed to do any damage. At 0300 hours on 25 October the destroyer divisions began their attacks. The Japanese were sailing in a straight line with the destroyers *Michishio, Asagumo, Shigure,* and *Yamagumo* in front, followed by *Yamashiro, Fuso,* and *Mogami.* The *Fuso* was hit first, dropped out of line, and began to burn and explode. The *Yamashiro* was hit twice, and all the destroyers except *Shigure* were sunk or disabled. None of the American destroyers was damaged. Nishimura, now left with only three ships – *Yamashiro, Mogami,* and *Shigure,* plowed straight ahead toward his objective, neither ordering evasive action nor taking any notice of his damaged ships.

The formidable American battle line (three heavy and two light cruisers on the left, one heavy and two light cruisers on the right, and six battleships with a destroyer screen in the center) stretched across the mouth of the Strait; and as the three Japanese ships approached, Oldendorf found himself in the same position as if he were crossing the Japanese T. In other words, he could turn his ships at right angles to the approaching enemy and rake them with devastating broadsides, to which the Japanese could only reply with the forward guns. The American line opened fire at 0351 hours. *California*, *Tennessee*, and *West Virginia*, who were equipped with the new Mark 8 fire control radar, scored most of the hits. The other battleships, with the old Mark 3 radar, had trouble finding targets. In 18 minutes the American ships fired almost 300 14 inch and 16 inch shells. The Japanese ships died slowly, and their commanders bravely carried on while their ships were blasted from beneath them.

At 0355 hours, *Mogami*, burning fiercely but still firing and launching torpedoes, reversed course and began to move south; just after 0400 hours her bridge was shelled, killing the commander and his staff and bringing the ship to a halt. By this time, the *Yamashiro* had also turned south and was burning brightly against the night sky. As the American battleships moved in for the kill, two torpedoes from the destroyer *Newcombe* hit and the old battleship quickly sank.

Admiral Shima, following with the Second

Striking Force, had intercepted messages from Nishimura as early as midnight that warned him he was in for a fight. At 0300 hours he turned north into the strait, already able to see flashes of gunfire from the battle ahead. An American PT boat patrolling the channel knocked the light cruiser *Abakuma* out of formation with a torpedo. Undaunted, Shima carried on. Half an hour later he passed the burning *Fuso* which had broken in half. He took the two hulks, which were silhouetted by their own flames, to be two ships – the *Fuso* and the *Yamashiro* – and his fears increased. Next he came upon the *Shigure*, heading south, and then *Mogami*, apparently dead in the water. The radar showed a group of American ships some six to eight miles north of *Mogami*. Shima ordered an attack and the *Nachi* and *Ashigara* swung over. But *Mogami* was not standing still – she was actually creeping south at about eight knots, being desperately navigated

from her engine room. *Ashigara* managed to avoid a collision but the flagship *Nachi*, in the lead, collided with the *Mogami* and tore a hole in her own bow. Meanwhile Shima's four destroyers had failed to make contact with the Americans. Shima decided that to continue north would be folly, and just before 0500 hours the entire force, including the crippled *Mogami*, began to withdraw. As dawn appeared Oldendorf began a general pursuit down the strait with nearly a score of cruisers and destroyers. The *Mogami* and the destroyer *Asagumo* were sunk; the *Abakuma* went down the following day. Protection of the Leyte beach-head was still the Seventh Fleet's primary concern, however, and Oldendorf decided to break off the pursuit. Shima's remaining two heavy cruisers and two destroyers made it to safety as did *Shigure*, the only survivor of Nishima's force.

While the Battle of the Surigao Strait was

going on, Admiral Kurita was cautiously working his way down the 150-mile length of the San Bernardino Strait. His crews were at battle stations, the lookouts tensely straining their eyes for the first sign of the enemy – but no enemy appeared. Halsey, who believed Kurita to be in retreat, had come to the conclusion that Center Force was no longer a serious threat. He had then taken the entire Third Fleet north to chase Ozawa's decoy force, without alerting Kinkaid to Kurita's presence or leaving a single ship to patrol the San Bernardino Strait. Both Kinkaid and Nimitz, however, believed that Halsey had left a force of heavy ships to block the entrance to Leyte Gulf.

They were soon to learn otherwise. At sunrise on 25 October Kurita emerged from the strait and discovered a group of carriers dead ahead. At 0648 hours, thinking he had stumbled across Mitscher's Task Force 38, he opened fire. The crews of what was actually the escort carrier group Taffy 3, under the command of Rear

Admiral Sprague, were taken completely by surprise as they ate breakfast on what was to have been another routine day.

Taffy 3 was one of three elements, or units, in Rear Admiral Thomas Sprague's Task Group 77.4. Each unit consisted of four to six escort carriers or CVEs, three destroyers, and four lightly armed destroyer-escorts. Until now they had been flying routine support missions for the Leyte landings. Each carrier normally had a complement of 18 Wildcats and 12 Avengers.

They were vulnerable targets: small, slow, unarmored, and lightly gunned craft. If the handsome big carriers got most of the glory, the little escort carriers handled more of the tedious, day-to-day routine. Often called 'jeep carriers' or 'baby flattops,' they had many other names as well – of which 'bucket of bolts' is the most polite. Many crewmen insisted that CVE really stood for 'Combustible, Vulnerable, Expendable,' and indeed the little carriers were never designed for a stand-up fight.

ABOVE: *Landing on a carrier was by no means easy even in calm weather as this aircraft shows with the pilot clearly turning away to try again.*

RIGHT: *Aircraft are hastily prepared for take-off while in the background Japanese shells land around a sister escort carrier during the crisis moments at Leyte Gulf.*

As the shells began to splash around his ships, Sprague, a former carrier commander in the Battle of the Philippine Sea, launched whatever planes he had on board. Then the group sped off at the maximum CVE speed, sending out urgent, plain-language calls for help. Taffys 1 and 2 launched their own planes in support. Kinkaid, who up until that time had believed the Third Fleet was covering the San Bernardino Strait, could not help – the Seventh Fleet had yet to re-fill its ammunition lockers after the Battle in the Surigao Strait. Halsey was much too far away to do any good; although he ordered planes from Admiral McCain's task force to assist, it would be hours before they would arrive.

The Japanese made their first mistake when, in the excitement of the moment, they believed they were seeing carriers instead of escort car-riers, cruisers instead of destroyers, and des-troyers instead of destroyer escorts. The second mistake came when Kurita, instead of forming a battle line with his heavy ships and sending his destroyers in for torpedo attacks, ordered General Attack. This meant every ship for itself, and threw the Japanese force into confusion.

Sprague, faced with 'the ultimate in desperate circumstances,' formed his carriers in a rough circle surrounded by the destroyers and des-troyer escorts. As the Japanese ships closed in 'with disconcerting rapidity,' he ordered a tor-pedo attack to divert them and turned the car-riers south-southwest to get nearer Leyte.

Although they had twice the speed, the Japanese ships were unable to close in on the escort carriers, for the tenacious defense put up by Taffy 3's planes and destroyers forced them

into constant evasive action. Both planes and destroyers attacked over and over again until their ammunition was gone – and then made dry runs to divert Japanese fire from the carriers.

The bombers managed to put one heavy cruiser, *Suzuya*, out of commission early in the battle, and later sank two other cruisers. One of the destroyers, the *Johnston*, forced the heavy cruiser *Kumano* out of the fighting before being hit herself by three 14-inch and three 6-inch shells. Even when her power was gone and her engine room out she continued to fight, firing her guns manually, until three cruisers came up and blasted her until she had to be abandoned. Meanwhile the other two destroyers, *Hoel* and *Heermann*, carried on the battle. *Hoel* finally sank, having been hit 40 times.

Despite the efforts of their defenders, the American carriers were taking a pounding; the *Gambier Bay* was sunk at 0907 hours, and the *Kalinin Bay* took 13 hits from 8-inch guns. Then at 1230 hours Kurita broke off the action and began to retire; not realizing the damage his cruisers were beginning to inflict on the carriers, he had decided to reassemble his force and make another attempt to get into Leyte Gulf. Just then he learned of Southern Force's defeat in the Surigao Strait. As he turned away, 70 Avengers and Wildcats from Taffy 2 and 3 arrived and a signalman on the bridge of Sprague's flagship shouted 'Goddammit boys, they're getting away.'

Getting away they were, and just in time – Oldendorf's battleships were waiting for them at the mouth of Leyte Gulf, while both Task Force 38 and land-based planes were being prepared

ABOVE: *A Japanese Yokosuka Judy photographed seconds before crashing onto the deck of the carrier* Essex, *25 November 1944.*

RIGHT: *The conquest of Luzon. As during the Japanese offensive in 1941, the principal American landings were made in Lingayen Gulf.*

BELOW: *General MacArthur and General Stilwell. Stilwell had held positions in China and Burma for most of the war but was transferred to the Pacific in 1945.*

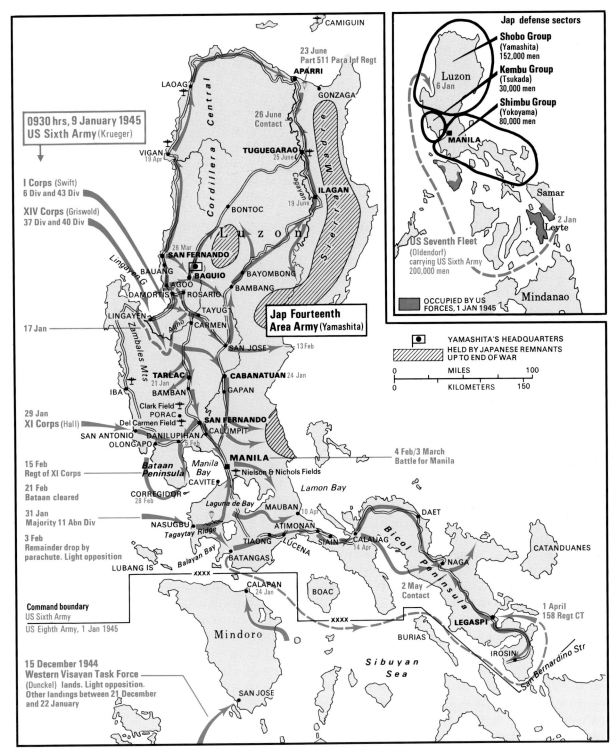

0930 hrs, 9 January 1945 US Sixth Army (Krueger)

I Corps (Swift)
6 Div and 43 Div

XIV Corps (Griswold)
37 Div and 40 Div

17 Jan

29 Jan
XI Corps (Hall)

15 Feb
Regt of XI Corps

21 Feb
Bataan cleared

31 Jan
Majority 11 Abn Div

3 Feb
Remainder drop by parachute. Light opposition

Command boundary
US Sixth Army
US Eighth Army, 1 Jan 1945

**15 December 1944
Western Visayan Task Force**
(Dunckel) lands. Light opposition.
Other landings between 21 December and 22 January

Jap Fourteenth Area Army (Yamashita)

Jap defense sectors
Shobo Group
(Yamashita)
152,000 men
Kembu Group
(Tsukada)
30,000 men
Shimbu Group
(Yokoyama)
80,000 men

US Seventh Fleet
(Oldendorf)
carrying US Sixth Army
200,000 men

OCCUPIED BY US FORCES, 1 JAN 1945

YAMASHITA'S HEADQUARTERS
HELD BY JAPANESE REMNANTS UP TO END OF WAR

4 Feb/3 March
Battle for Manila

2 May
Contact

1 April
158 Regt CT

---

for a massive air attack. Had he not turned back, Kurita would have shared Nishimura's fate. As it was, the most powerful force Japan had been able to amass since Midway had been turned back by a small, weak, relatively defenseless, but determined squadron – demonstrating the vulnerability of capital ships without air cover.

But the Taffys' troubles were not yet over. On 25 October Taffy 1 became the first American force to endure a kamikaze attack, and later the same day Taffy 3 was attacked eight times and the *St Lo* was sunk. The kamikazes were a special air corps, organized in a last desperate attempt to

make up for Japan's rapidly dwindling air power. In addition, obsolete planes and untrained pilots could be used. Vice-Admiral Onishi of First Air Fleet had already begun training a kamikaze corps when Rear Admiral Arima attempted the first deliberate kamikaze attack against the carrier *Franklin* on 15 October, and thousands of young Japanese volunteered to sacrifice their lives for the Emperor.

Meanwhile, Halsey and the powerful Third Fleet, who had been assigned to 'cover and support' the Army and to 'destroy enemy naval and air forces in or threatening the Philippines' were somewhere off Cape Engaño. Although the first duty of a covering force in an amphibious operation is to protect the landing force, Halsey saw his primary objective as the destruction of the Japanese fleet – and indeed his orders (which he had helped draft) gave him this option.

The Northern Force under Admiral Ozawa had left the Inland Sea on schedule, taking a course that would allow them to be seen – but not too soon. Ozawa had one fleet carrier and three light carriers with a total of only 116 planes between them, two 'hermaphrodite' carriers (battleships with cut-down superstructures to make room for a short flight deck), and a screen of three light cruisers and nine destroyers. On the morning of 24 October search planes discovered part of Task Force 38, and Ozawa sent out 76 planes to attack it. Only 29 returned. Finally, at 1540 hours, American search planes located the Japanese carrier force; the report, however, did not reach Halsey until 1700 hours.

Hearing of the sighting, the aggressive Halsey was galvanized into action – and into a critical error of judgement. Dismissing Kurita's force from his mind he ordered all 64 ships and 787 planes of the Third Fleet in pursuit of Ozawa's 17 ships and 116 planes.

At 0430 hours on the morning of 25 October Halsey launched his planes against the Japanese, who were reported to be 200 miles off Cape Engaño on Luzon. The first strike came in at 0845 hours – first the Helldivers, then the strafing Wildcats, and finally the Avengers sweeping in to release their torpedoes. Three more major strikes followed. Without a Combat Air Patrol, Ozawa was forced to rely on evasive tactics and anti-aircraft fire. Nevertheless, all four carriers and a destroyer went down during these strikes.

Halsey began getting calls for help from Taffy 3 at 0820 hours, but made no real move to send assistance; he wanted to keep his entire battle force with him to clean up the Japanese 'cripples' after the air strikes and to chase the two battleship carriers. He changed his mind, however, around 1000 hours when even Nimitz began asking what he was doing and what provision had been made to guard the San Bernardino Strait. At 1115 hours he sent one carrier group and most of the battle line south – much too late to be of any real help.

The remaining cruisers and destroyers followed Northern Force, finishing off a light cruiser and a large destroyer; but one light cruiser, the two battleship carriers, and five destroyers managed to escape. Ozawa, who was considered the ablest Japanese admiral after Yamamoto, had managed to save both Center Force and Northern Force from annihilation, despite the fact that he had 'expected complete destruction' on the mission. Halsey, on the other hand, had piled error upon error. The first, of course, was rising to the bait at all. The second was failing to leave a strong force to block the strait or at least to tell Kinkaid that it was unguarded. The third was his failure to retain a sufficient force to complete the destruction of Ozawa's force at the very end.

By 26 October the battle was over. The Allies had lost a light carrier, two escort carriers, two destroyers, and a destroyer escort. The Japanese were down three battleships, one fleet carrier, three light carriers, six heavy cruisers, four light cruisers, and nine destroyers. The two high points of the battle were Oldendorf's disposition of the Seventh Fleet in the night battle in the Surigao Strait and Ozawa's execution of his decoy mission. The low points were the Allies' failure to destroy either Center Force or Northern Force, and Kurita's failure to sink all of Taffy 3, which he might have done had he been able to retain tactical control of his force.

The greatest weakness on the American side was the divided command at the top. If one commander, whether MacArthur or Nimitz, had been in overall control, Halsey could not have decamped as he did without asking permission.

There are many reasons for the Japanese defeat: the overwhelming complexity of *Sho-1*; bad co-ordination between commanders; their inability, despite their bravery and competence, to alter their tactics to suit the circumstances; and perhaps most important, the lack of air power. If Leyte Gulf holds one great lesson, it is the helplessness of a modern fleet without air cover.

Leyte Gulf was the last main fleet action in history – and in view of the revolutionary changes in naval warfare, is likely to remain so. It is perhaps fitting then that it was also the last engagement of a battle line, a tactical device for naval combat that was first used successfully in the Battle of Lowestoft in 1655. As Oldendorf crossed the T at the mouth of Surigao Strait the battle line went into oblivion along with the Greek phalanx and the English longbow.

Although battleship tactics began to change early in the twentieth century with the development of the mine, torpedo, and submarine, the battleship itself remained the backbone of every navy until well into World War II. Between 1939 and 1945, however, the carrier came into its own; and by the Battle of Midway, as we have seen, it had become the dominant factor in naval warfare. For the rest of the war, battleships – at least

ABOVE: *Landing craft approach the beach at Leyte.*

RIGHT: *General MacArthur makes his triumphal and long-promised return to the Philippines. When MacArthur first came ashore on Leyte an overworked beachmaster (the officer responsible for all movements near the beach whom not even a supreme commander could overrule) gave orders for the general's party to land in this uncomfortable way. The scene was shot by a nearby cameraman, MacArthur realized the appeal of the picture and re-enacted the episode for further photos of which the example here is one.*

in the American navy – were assigned support roles for carriers and amphibious landings.

Although the naval Battle of Leyte Gulf was over, the land fighting for the Philippines clearly had a long way to go. We have already seen how substantial US forces had gone ashore successfully in the first couple of days of landings but what were the Japanese ready to do to oppose them on land?

Defending the Philippines as a whole, General Yamashita Tomoyuki had about 350,000 men at his disposal. Some of these were needed to deal with the Filipino guerrillas, and the rest were distributed through the islands. On Leyte itself the Japanese had only one division, totalling about 16,000 men, and by the end of the month the Americans had occupied most of the northern part of the island. But by this time Yamashita had ordered his Thirty-Fifth Army to move to Leyte, and 35,000 men were landed before the Americans cut the Japanese sea communications there.

The Japanese strategy was to concentrate in the mountainous central part of the island, out of range of the elderly US battleships whose heavy guns could be so destructive against coastal strongpoints. The stubborn Japanese resistance in this area was aided by heavy rainfall, which brought the American advance almost to a halt in November. A main Japanese base at Ormoc, covered by enemy troop concentrations in the nearby mountains, was attacked by the US XXIV Corps, but held out until the US 77th Division landed in an outflanking movement. The capture of Ormoc was followed by a link-up at Libungao of the two US prongs.

Cut off, the Japanese resisted a little longer, but by the end of December, short of food, they were disorganized and weak. Meanwhile, a beachhead on the neighbouring island of Samar had been established. Although there remained on Leyte a few scattered bands of Japanese, to all intents and purposes the island was in American hands from January 1945, opening the way for an attack on the largest island, Luzon. In the Leyte operations the Japanese lost about 70,000 men, more than four times the US casualties. Thus the high ratio of Japanese to American casualties continued, despite the general rule that attack is more costly than defense. The Japanese practice of fighting to the very end, together with overwhelming US air superiority, explains this.

Having conquered Leyte, General Mac-Arthur turned his attention to the main island of the Philippines, Luzon. Some 850 ships were provided by the US Seventh Fleet to convey 200,000 men from Leyte to the Lingayen Gulf.

LEFT: *A US flamethrower operator moves in on Japanese positions at Clark Field on the outskirts of Manila.*

BELOW RIGHT: *Men of the 145th Infantry outside Manila's main Post Office during the final stages of the fighting for the city.*

BELOW: *MacArthur inspects the ruins of the Manila Hotel which had been his home before the war when he commanded the forces in the Philippines.*

Supported by gunfire from Seventh Fleet battleships and by aircraft from Halsey's Third Fleet, the landings were made in two thrusts, each by two divisions. On the way in, however, the ships were subjected to severe attacks by suicide pilots who would have caused really crucial losses had they not, in the Japanese martial tradition, directed themselves against warships rather than the more vulnerable troopships.

General Yamashita had divided his defending Fourteenth Army into three parts, with the largest part in the north. He made no attempt to defend the beaches, knowing that his men would be crushed by naval gunfire. Instead, he intended to fight a stubborn campaign in the interior, retiring eventually into the mountains. The first US landings were made on 6 January, and by 23 January one corps had reached the Clark Field airbase. The US Eighth Army, which had been sent to clear the southern islands, was then diverted to Luzon, where it captured Olongapo and cut off the Bataan Peninsula. Yamashita, however, had made sure that few of his forces would be left in that peninsula. Other US divisions were landed south of Manila, the intention being to advance on that capital from north and south.

Yamashita, wisely preferring to conserve his strength, did not intend to fight for Manila, but his subordinate there, an admiral commanding 18,000 sailors, decided that a heroic last stand would be more seemly than a withdrawal. So, for the first and only time in the Pacific campaign, American troops were forced into a major urban battle, fighting from street to street and house to house. This struggle lasted two weeks; it cost the Americans 1000 dead but the local Filipino civilians suffered more, with perhaps 100,000 killed as their city was progressively burned and destroyed around them. Before the Americans could use the magnificent Manila harbor, Corregidor had to be captured, and this was done with seaborne and airborne landings, followed by ten days of bloody fighting.

Yamashita fought on. In May, although southern Luzon was in American hands, the Japanese were still strong in the north, in the Sierra Madre and Cordillera Central mountains. How long the Japanese could have held out was never tested, because when Japan made peace in August, Yamashita, still with 50,000 troops at his disposal, surrendered.

7.
China – Burma – India

As the Japanese onslaught against the Western colonial powers in Asia began to wind down in the spring of 1942, the Fifteenth Army under General Iida Shojiro found itself firmly in control of the British colony of Burma. British command in India had officially abandoned the country at the end of April, leaving only a portion of the far north, held by Chin and Kachin tribesmen, out of Japanese hands. As the British had made no particular provision for the defense of Burma, Iida's troops, aided by a population largely hostile to British rule, had had an easy campaign. Yet Burma was not to be quickly overrun and then forgotten – a backwater on the periphery of the war – but was instead to remain an area of intense combat throughout the war years.

A transit area between China and India, Burma had been invaded by the Japanese primarily to secure the southwest flank of China. After seizing the main population areas of China in 1937-38, the Japanese had not deemed it wise to attempt to pursue the forces of the Kuomintang leader Chiang Kai-shek into the mountainous interior of the country. The immediate strategy was to cut the routes over which foreign supplies reached Chiang at his base of Chungking. The 1941 non-aggression pact between Japan and the Soviet Union ended Soviet aid to China, while the occupation of French Indochina in 1940 closed the road and rail route from Hanoi to Kunming. A marginal amount of supplies had come in via the British colony of Hong Kong which fell in December 1941, but the most important route was the road between Kunming in Yunnan in southwest China and Lashio in northern Burma, hewed by hand by 100,000 Chinese coolies in 1937 and 1938. Supplies were docked in Rangoon, shipped up the Irrawaddy River to Lashio and thence to China over what came to be known as the Burma Road. This supply route was so important to China that Chiang

volunteered his best troops, the German-trained Fifth and Sixth Armies, for the defense of Burma in 1942. This move did not forestall the loss of Burma and the closing of the Burma Road, but it did cost Chiang his armies which were shattered in the campaign.

Japan also had no designs on India at this time but had wished to include the important rice exporting country of Burma within the new 'Greater East Asia Co-prosperity Sphere'. The modest British and Indian forces in India were demoralized and ill-equipped and were considered to present little threat. The pestilential border area between Burma and India was thought to constitute a natural barrier as it had few communications. Posting troops to guard the several possible approaches from India, the Japanese in Burma were content to remain on the defensive after the spring of 1942, even shifting some of their air power from Burma to the campaigns in the Pacific.

The Japanese in Burma had little to fear in 1942 as the war priorities of the Allies had placed Europe first, the Pacific second, and what was termed the 'China-Burma-India Theater' or CBI last. China was now completely isolated and no longer taking an active part in the war. Having borne the brunt of the war with Japan since 1937, the Kuomintang under Chiang Kai-shek believed that China had already done its share and that the war would be won elsewhere by China's new allies, Britain and the United States. Prime Minister Winston Churchill had little respect for the corrupt government of Chiang or for China's military capacity and, once Burma had fallen, had no other interest beyond regaining Burma and Malaya. The British were therefore quite unsympathetic to the American determination to break the blockade of China and ultimately to use China as a base against Japan. Thus British aims in the CBI were much more limited than those of their American allies.

BELOW: *Japanese troops with a group of Chinese shortly to be executed. Japanese rule in their occupied territories and their treatment of prisoners was very harsh.*

While the immediate efforts of the Americans were directed toward opening an air supply route from northeast India to China, the immediate British interest was to strike in Burma as quickly as possible.

Whether it was launching the air supply route over the 'hump' or launching, however limited, an offensive against Burma, India was a difficult base from which to attempt either. An agricultural land with a population of over 400 million already on the verge of famine, India had no surplus capacity for military effort and could not be an important source of supplies. India also lay 12,000 miles from the main source of supplies, which was the United States. After over two months in transit from America, supplies had to be docked at Bombay and Karachi on the west coast of India and trans-shipped 1500 miles to eastern India and Assam where the forward Allied air bases and defenses lay. Heat, dust, disease and bad food made India and Assam an extremely difficult and debilitating environment for occidental troops. Accepting the opportunity offered by the war, the Indian nationalist movement under Mohandas K. Gandhi was undertaking a campaign of civil disobedience which led to widespread strife and sabotage.

The most formidable problem faced by the Allies in India was the fact that the Indian transportation system was wholly inadequate for moving large quantities of supplies from western

ABOVE: *Massed
manpower prepares an
airfield for American
planes in China,
1943.*

LEFT: *General Claire
Chennault had led the
American Volunteer
Air Group assisting
the Chinese
Nationalists before the
war. During the war
he continued to
command USAAF
forces in China.*

RIGHT: *Major John Herbst, a leading ace with the Fourteenth Air Force in China.*

BELOW: *A group of pilots run to their P-40 fighters. Their aircraft are painted with the shark's mouth insignia previously used by the American Volunteer Group.*

LEFT: *General Wingate (4th from left) and a group of Chindit officers.*

India to Assam. The road system was simply undeveloped. Motor transport could not seriously be considered, even if there had been a sufficient number of trucks. The burden, therefore, fell on the rail system which was subject to numerous delays and breakdowns under the new wartime requirements. The initial problem was somewhat alleviated by a trans-India air cargo service, and by 1943 it was possible to bring in supplies through Calcutta on the eastern coast of India as the Japanese naval threat in the Bay of Bengal had receded. A large program to construct pipelines and improve the Assam-Bengal Railway up the Brahmaputra Valley had to be launched with all the attendant difficulties of any wartime project in India. Until these logistic improvements could be made, the flow of supplies over the hump to China would be a trickle and the British ability to strike at Burma would remain limited. The overall question was that although the Allies paid lip service to the importance of China and Burma, the CBI in practice enjoyed the lowest priority of all the Allied theaters of the war in the allocation of resources, a fact which meant that CBI remained starved of men and matériel throughout the war.

CBI was primarily a British and Chinese theater. For the United States, it was almost entirely an air rather than a ground theater as there were never more than a few thousand American ground troops in CBI, mainly OSS and commando units such as Merrill's Marauders. For most of the war American troops in the theater came under the command of General Joseph 'Vinegar Joe' Stilwell, a tough and able fighter who never quite grasped the nature of his mission in CBI. The American units under his command were the Tenth American Air Force in India and the China Air Task Force at Kunming under Claire Chennault. Chennault had left the US Air Force in 1937 to serve as an adviser to the air force of Chiang Kai-shek. He had subsequently been asked to form a group of mercenary pilots for the air defense of China. The new American Volunteer Group saw its first action in the defense of Burma. In conjunction with a few British squadrons, the AVG had fought well against overwhelming opposition, downing four and five Japanese planes for each AVG plane lost. After the fall of Burma, the AVG had moved to Kunming where it constituted China's only air defense against the Japanese. In July 1942 the AVG was incorporated into the US Army Air Force as the China Air Task Force and subsequently became the US Fourteenth Air Force.

As Chief of Staff of the Nationalist Chinese Armies, Stilwell also had control of the Chinese troops who had escaped from Burma to India. These were now being retrained and re-equipped at Ramgarh while more Chinese troops were being assembled in Yunnan for the same purpose.

RIGHT: *Sick and wounded Chindits are evacuated for medical treatment.*

BELOW: *A Hurricane fighter-bomber being armed for a mission over the Arakan in late 1943. By this time the Allies were commanding the air over Burma.*

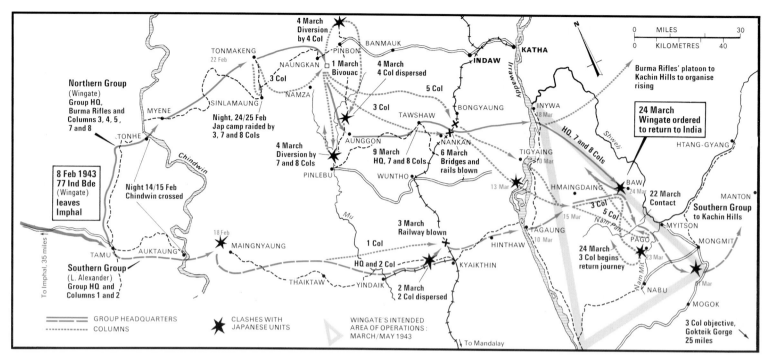

ABOVE: *The Chindit operations in Burma in 1943. Casualties to the Chindit force were heavy, many of them through disease, and their concrete achievements were limited but their efforts did raise morale in other units in Burma by helping to prove that the Japanese were not invincible in the jungle.*

LEFT: *The relief force finally joins up with the Imphal garrison, 22 June 1944.*

ABOVE RIGHT: *Chindit soldiers from a variety of units wait to be airlifted forward to the 'Broadway' base during the second Chindit expedition in March 1944.*

RIGHT: *The Allied Supreme Commander in South-East Asia, Admiral Lord Mountbatten, addresses men of the US 1st Air Commando.*

British headquarters in India had fifteen divisions available after the end of the Burma retreat, but most were newly formed and lacked equipment, training and experienced officers. Only three divisions were actually in any condition to undertake operations. In April 1942 the British commander, General Sir Archibald Wavell, organized his forces into three regional commands, with Eastern Command under General Noel Irwin the operational one. The Allied position was improving in at least one respect, however, as a flow of new aircraft was redressing the Japanese superiority in air power. Fortunately for the Allies, the Japanese were never motivated to launch a sustained air offensive against Assam and northeast India but made only a few sporadic raids in 1942 which went virtually unopposed.

In October 1942 Chiang put forward a plan for

LEFT: *Lieutenant General Scoones commanded IV Corps during that formation's encirclement at Imphal.*

BELOW: *General Slim (center) with (left) General Stopford and General Fowkes.*

Kawabe, the Japanese commander in Burma, aware that the Burma-India frontier was not impenetrable and that a British offensive was in the making.

Although various operations for Burma were under consideration during the rainy season of 1943, the logistic and administrative difficulties were much too great and all plans were shelved. Stilwell continued to train his Chinese troops in India and Yunnan while the US Air Force continued to build air fields and pipelines in India and Assam in an effort to get more supplies to China where Chennault was proposing an air offensive against the Japanese. Combined British and American efforts continued to improve the logistics between India and Assam. Guerrilla operations by tribesmen in North Burma were beginning while Allied intelligence became aware for the first time that the Burmese nationalists were disenchanted with their Japanese liberators and were organizing their own resistance movement. In military terms, however, the most important trend was that the RAF and the US Tenth Air Force were beginning to contest Japanese air superiority over

the reconquest of Burma. Chinese, British and Indian forces would strike from Assam while other Chinese forces advanced from Yunnan in a pincer movement. A seaborne attack was also to be made on Rangoon. The plan was much beyond British capabilities in air and manpower, but when Wavell pointed out its limitations, Chiang angrily withdrew. Under pressure from Churchill to take some action, Wavell attempted to recover part of the coast of Arakan with an advance by the 14th Indian Division. A neat Japanese counterstroke turned the effort into a dismal and costly failure by early 1943.

The next British effort against Burma was led by Brigadier Orde Wingate, a brilliant and unorthodox solider who advocated guerrilla warfare on the model of T.E. Lawrence and the Arab Revolt of World War I. Wavell approved a long range penetration by 3000 commandos, known as 'Chindits', to disrupt the enemy lines of communication. In a two-month operation of no strategic significance, Wingate temporarily put a Burmese railway out of action and lost a third of his men. Wingate was killed in a plane crash at the beginning of a second and larger operation in early 1944. As he had provided a model of exciting warfare with an emphasis on individual performance, the British propaganda machine overnight turned him into a hero. One of the more important results of the first Chindit operation, however, was that it made General

BELOW RIGHT: *Slim in conversation with a Gurkha rifleman. One of Slim's most important qualities was his ability to gain the respect and trust of the ordinary soldiers in his command.*

Burma. Throughout 1943 and into 1944 the struggle for the air increased in vigor. The continuing Allied build-up in India now made it evident that the Japanese forces in Burma could no longer safely remain on the defensive.

The Allies had now agreed that the conquest of North Burma must be a primary objective in order to reopen the Burma Road. The aim was to build up Chinese forces for an effort against the Japanese and to supply an offensive by the Fourteenth Air Force. Although not explicitly stated in Allied policy, it was expected that all of Burma would be cleared in the process. The CBI Theater had been reorganized with the Southeast Asia Command or SEAC under Admiral Lord Louis Mountbatten as the operational body. Stilwell now served as deputy to Mountbatten but also as Chinese Chief of Staff. Wavell was made Viceroy of India while the duties of Commander-in-Chief in India fell to Sir Claude Auchinleck. The newly-formed Fourteenth Army under General William Slim intended a limited offensive in Arakan as preparation for a subsequent and larger offensive to clear Burma. Slim's idea was to move into the jungle, create

strongholds supplied from the air, and then crush the counter-attacking enemy between these and his subsequent all-out drive. The air power to support this tactic was now available with 48 British and 19 American squadrons totalling around 850 planes. There were also now enough cargo planes for airborne supply operations while more could be borrowed from the India-China airlift. Operations were to begin in the dry season of 1944, concurrently with a pincer movement from Assam and Yunnan by Chinese troops under Stilwell.

The Allied offensive which was so obviously in preparation caused the Japanese to undertake a spoiling operation of their own. Realizing that they faced potential attack from fourteen divisions in China and from up to six in India, the Japanese planned to occupy the Imphal plain and thus deprive the Allies of their staging bases for attack on Burma and for support of China. Such a move would also cut off Stilwell's operations from supplies and reinforcements. Although this offensive was mainly preventive in its inspiration, there was a considerable propaganda fanfare about a 'march on Delhi' which stemmed from

the presence of the Indian National Army. Led by a 46-year-old former Mayor of Calcutta named Subhas Chandra Bose, the INA was the military arm of the Azad Hind or Free India movement among the overseas Indians in Southeast Asia (there were 800,000 Indians in Malaya alone). Bose dreamed of marching on Delhi at the head of his forces to liberate India from British rule, but the Japanese Army only wanted his men as guides, spies and liaison troops. In the end, the INA was allowed three fighting divisions of 2000 men each with the rest of its forces as auxiliary troops. The Japanese Army reserved for itself the right of gaining the first victory on Indian soil and intended to offer the capture of Imphal as a birthday present to the Emperor.

At the top of the Japanese command structure was General Kawabe, under whom were three armies: the 33rd under General Honda in the northeast, the 28th under General Sakurai on the Arakan front, and the 15th under General Mutaguchi on the central front. Each of these

armies was roughly equivalent to a British army corps. After preparatory attacks against Arakan and Yunnan, the drive on Imphal was to be launched by the forces of Mutaguchi.

In mid-March 1944 three Japanese divisions began their drive on Imphal, unaffected by a second and larger Chindit penetration into the valley of the Irrawaddy River. IV Corps of General Sir Geoffrey Scoones had already begun Allied operations by slowly moving southward from Imphal in three columns, but on receiving intelligence of the possibility of a Japanese offensive, it halted and took up defensive positions. The Japanese move actually cut off one of Scoones' divisions while a flanking advance from the Chindwin area was also forcing a British withdrawal in the north. A deep flanking movement then cut the Imphal-Kohima Road at the end of March and required the British to move up three fresh divisions from India. Four divisions were then deployed in defensive positions on the Imphal Plain, but

ABOVE: *A Lysander light scout aircraft being used on a supply dropping mission over Burma.*

ABOVE RIGHT: *A map of the fighting at Imphal.*

RIGHT: *British and Australian prisoners working in a lumber camp in Thailand. Conditions for prisoners working on the Burma-Thailand railroad were notoriously bad.*

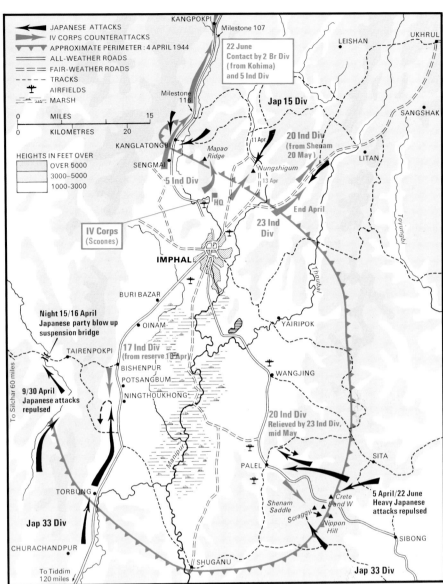

Kohima to the north was held by only 1500 men. The Dimapur-Kohima area was assigned to Lieutenant General Montagu Stopford and his XXXIII Corps, but the Japanese began their attack on Kohima on 4 April before the bulk of the corps had arrived from India.

The Kohima garrison suddenly found itself cut off from its reinforcements which in turn were cut off from their base at Dimapur. A general counteroffensive in the area was ordered by General Slim on 10 April. After heavy fighting two relieving brigades rescued the exhausted troops defending Kohima and began operations to clear the Japanese from the surrounding area.

The fighting around Kohima had been fierce but the struggle for Imphal surpassed it. The operations of the Third Tactical Air Force under Air Marshal Sir John Baldwin which were annihilating Japanese air strength in Burma became a key factor. For their Imphal campaign to have any chance of real success the Japanese had to throw the bulk of their air power into support.

Here the issue was decided as the 576 fighters and 149 bombers of the Allies destroyed 117 planes over Imphal and forced the Japanese air force into essentially defensive actions. Within two months another 85 Japanese planes had been downed, and Allied control of the air over Burma could no longer be challenged. This development meant that the Allies could make unrestricted use of air supply, first to keep the Imphal garrison alive during the Japanese siege, and subsequently to supply virtually their entire offensive in Burma as land communications were so execrable. As an added bonus, the hump airlift was now free from Japanese air harassment and greatly expanded its supply capacity for China.

Thus 28,000 British and 30,000 Indian troops endured a heavy siege at Imphal supplied entirely by air. The fighting at Imphal was characterized by hand to hand combat of such savagery that a Japanese journalist likened it to Verdun in World War I. Stopford's forces were pushing down the Imphal-Kohima Road by May, however, while Scoones' men were pressing from the south. At this point Mutaguchi could have withdrawn in good order and for good reasons. His troops were short of supplies and no longer had hope of receiving more as his makeshift lines of communication were long and ran through very difficult country. As the Japanese no longer had

any air cover, the supply lines had been cut by Allied air attacks in any event. Yet despite the deterioration in his position, Mutaguchi clung on to the siege of Imphal in spite of fierce dissent from his subordinates. He was soon driven to relieve all three of his divisional commanders in his obstinacy. The siege had been broken by late May and a general counterattack begun by Slim's forces. Starving and disease ridden, the remnants of the Japanese invading force were saved only by retreating into the monsoon.

General Kawabe had sent 85,000 men against India, but only 32,000 returned. The campaign has been so severe that for the first time in the war, Japanese morale cracked and some troops actually surrendered. Even measured against 16,700 British and Indian casualties, Imphal was the worst disaster suffered by the Japanese Army in World War II. A number of factors had contributed to create this débâcle. The loss of complete air superiority to the Allies was decisive. There had also been poor staff work on the part of an army not familiar with campaigning in the tropics. The only large scale tropical campaign fought by the Japanese Army had been in Malaya. Most training was still geared to temperate climates. The favored tactic of forcing the enemy to retreat by hooking movements around his flanks had failed for the first time after its brilliant use in the Burma and Malaya campaigns

of 1942. Slim's tactics were not to retreat but, relying on air supply, to stand and fight. On the basis of the British and Indian performance in Malaya, a gross underestimation of the fighting ability of the enemy had led to supreme overconfidence on the part of the Japanese. Incidentally, the INA had mostly deserted when the shooting began. Bose was discredited and subsequently died in a plane crash while trying to escape to the Soviet Union.

On 3rd June 1944 the Combined Chiefs of Staff ordered Mountbatten to improve the air link with China and re-open the Burma Road. With high hopes Stilwell had opened a limited offensive in North Burma with Chinese troops in February. One force was slowly pushing into the Hukawng Valley from Ledo in Assam, building a road as it proceeded. Another force was reluctantly advancing from Yunnan and making slow progress. Under the new Combined Chiefs of Staff directive, Stilwell's mission was to clear north Burma while Slim's forces seized Rangoon to force a Japanese evacuation of south Burma. The overall role of the China Theater was now to support the coming Allied offensives in the Pacific. This could only be accomplished by Chennault's Fourteenth Air Force, which needed an augmented airlift and the re-opening of the Burma Road. Stilwell's forces managed to capture the key airfield at Myitkyina in May but

ABOVE: *Crossing the Irrawaddy, February 1945. A Sherman tank follows a scout car.*

ABOVE LEFT: *DUKW amphibians bring supplies across the Chindwin, January 1945.*

LEFT: *A further photograph illustrating the importance of well-planned river crossing operations during the final campaign in Burma. Here a Bren carrier has been fitted with empty drums as a flotation aid.*

1944. The intervening period was used to re-organize for the coming operations. Because the land communications of Burma were so poor, all operations depended on air supply; thus this key function was centralized under a command designated as the Combat Cargo Task Force. The 'Special Force' units were disbanded while the intelligence services were better coordinated. Some changes in command were made as well. General Sir Oliver Leese was made Commander-in-Chief of Allied Land Forces, Southeast Asia, under Mountbatten.

The most significant change in command came in the month that the new operations were to begin. Stilwell had been a controversial figure in CBI and in the Allied councils of war since his appointment as theater commander in 1942. Through no fault of Stilwell's the Japanese had shattered his Chinese forces in the invasion of Burma in that year. He was a soldier's soldier who wanted desperately to fight to redeem himself, but there was little fighting to be done. Stilwell never accepted the fact that what the Allies required of China was not offensives against the enemy but only survival. His relationship with Chiang was acrimonious largely because of his frustration at Chiang's refusal to fight any more than when it was absolutely necessary. Stilwell was in conflict with Chennault over the allocation of the modest tonnage flown at great cost over the hump. The former wanted equipment for his Yunnan force to invade Burma while the latter needed gasoline and bombs for the planes of his Fourteenth Air Force. Allied strategists tended to favor Chennault's proposals for air offensives against Japan over Stilwell's costly and myopic plans to clear North Burma, reopen the Burma Road, and build up the Chinese armies to drive Japan from China. The politics surrounding the blunt personality of Stilwell finally angered Chiang to the point of demanding his recall. General Albert Wedemeyer, a man of more diplomatic mien, replaced Stilwell as Chief of Staff to Chiang and subsequently achieved some more tangible results through better working relationships with the Chinese.

When the rains let up in October 1944, the Burma Area Army under General Kimura was ordered to block the Allied offensive to prevent the re-opening of the Burma Road for an attack from Burma on Malaya. With General MacArthur and Admiral Nimitz attacking Leyte in the Philippines that same month, there were, of course, to be no reinforcements for Burma. Japanese strength in Burma had been shattered by the débâcle at Imphal. There was only one division in southern Burma to cover Rangoon

failed to conquer the town itself until August. The capture of the airfield assisted the airlift greatly as Myitkyina could now be used as a base as well as the southern and easier route over the hump to China. The Burma Road never did regain its place as the primary supply route for China, however, since Lashio was not recaptured until January 1945 and after that, the road was only used for the one-way delivery of vehicles and artillery to China. The Ledo Road was used to supply the Myitkyina area, and that town was quickly turned into a major supply depot for the campaign to clear the remainder of Burma.

Following the Japanese defeat at Imphal, two plans were developed by Mountbatten and Slim to destroy the Japanese hold on Burma. 'Dracula' was an amphibious operation against southern Burma, but since it required outside supplies such as landing craft, it was given lower priority than 'Capital', an overland drive into north-central Burma. The plan was that once on the central plain of Burma, Slim's tanks, artillery and air power could be used to maximum effect against the enemy. Operations could not begin until the dry season recommenced in October while four divisions of the Fifteenth Army faced nine strong British and Indian divisions. Other Japanese forces were attempting to hold the Chinese troops under Wedemeyer moving south from Myitkyina towards Lashio and the Burma Road. There was little air cover for the Japanese forces. In all, Kimura realized how poor his prospects were and knew that the Japanese position in north Burma was probably untenable, but he still hoped to hold a line across Mandalay and the Yenangyaung oil fields.

In mid-November the XXXIII Corps of Stopford and the IV Corps of Messervy were over the Chindwin River, hoping to encircle the Japanese forces defending the Shwebo Plain. The Japanese withdrew on Mandalay, hence Slim sent Messervy due south to cut their communications with Rangoon and block their retreat. By March the Japanese were under serious pressure at Mandalay and had abandoned north Burma to Wedemeyer's advance. It was at Mandalay that the Japanese suffered their first attack from disenchanted Burmese nationalist forces, which at this point were also prepared to fight the returning British. The troops at Mandalay fought doggedly, repulsing repeated British attacks, while a counteroffensive was launched against Messervy around Meiktila. But the counteroffensive failed and Mandalay fell to Stopford's troops on 20 March. What was left of the Fifteenth Army retreated to the south as best it could, leaving central Burma to the victorious British and the road to Rangoon open.

Slim now decreed that Messervy's corps was to drive on Rangoon along the main road and rail route while Stopford did the same along both banks of the Irrawaddy. The former would continue to be supplied by air while the latter was to be sustained by riverine transport. Time was pressing, however, as the monsoon was due in May and would curtail the air supply on which the entire campaign had thus far depended. China was also in crisis, hence many of the cargo planes on which Slim depended were due to be shifted there in June. It was imperative, therefore, that Rangoon be secured before the monsoon broke. Operation Dracula thus was put into effect as insurance on 1 May by a British division, a tank regiment and a Gurkha parachute battalion. The Japanese had evacuated Rangoon during the last week of April, enabling the British to enter the city on 2 May unopposed. The city was in fact already under the control of Burmese nationalist troops under the then Colonel Ne Win. Four days later, the troops of Operation Dracula met advance units of Messervy's force moving south.

ABOVE: *An older form of transport with the Royal Scots during the capture of Mandalay.*

LEFT: *A Sherman tank pushes through the town of Pegu on 1 May 1945 during the last days of fighting in Burma.*

The Burma campaign was essentially completed with the recapture of Rangoon. General Bill Slim had gained a complete and decisive victory, destroying three Japanese armies in the field during a brilliantly executed campaign. The Japanese generals and their men had fought tenaciously, but lacking air cover and supply, they were no match for the well-equipped and supplied Allied troops. The Japanese had also had to contend with the mainline Burmese resistance (as opposed to the guerrillas of the hill areas). Frustrated with the Japanese failure to allow true independence, the mainline Burmese nationalists had been cooperating with the British Force 136 since late 1943 and had launched a full scale offensive against the Japanese in March 1945. The nationalist leader Aung San had reached an accommodation with Slim and Mountbatten which prevented hostilities between the returning British and the well organized and armed nationalists. Burma subsequently achieved her long-sought independence through negotiation rather than armed struggle.

Well before the Burma campaign got underway in the fall of 1944, the other combat area of CBI suddenly flared up with major offensives by the Japanese in China. After halting major operations against Chiang Kai-shek in 1938, the Japanese had been largely quiescent, preferring to blockade China and trying to draw Chiang into a separate peace to take China out of the war. It was thought that the constant strain of war and of the confrontation with the Communist forces of Mao Tse-tung in north China would sooner or later bring Chiang to the negotiating table. And indeed, between 1938 and 1944, there were steady defections to the Japanese and the collaborationist government of Wang Ching-wei. The Chinese Communists, for example, estimated that no fewer than 27 Kuomintang generals changed sides. China not only had to cope with over a million Japanese troops but also with the continuing civil war between Chiang's Nationalists and Mao's Communists. Chiang employed 200,000 of his best troops to cordon off the Communist area around Yenan and blocked any American aid to Mao. The Communists for their part were eventually able to carry out some limited guerrilla warfare and to restrict the Japanese in their area increasingly to the towns while slowly bringing more and more of the countryside under their control.

Thus, from 1938 to 1944 the war in China was characterized by sporadic small-scale actions of minor military consequence. Occupying the cities and major towns, the Japanese were harassed by guerrilla activity and in many places could only venture into the countryside in great force. In return, the Japanese carried out sporadic raids and did much damage to the countryside. In some parts of the country, there was no fighting and the opponents reached a profitable modus vivendi through small scale trade. The Japanese Navy in particular was noted for its trafficking with the Chinese. Little territory had changed hands since 1938 in this stalemated war.

It was neither the Chinese nor the Japanese but the Americans who caused the stalemate in China to end. As the amount of supplies that could be flown over the hump increased, the Fourteenth Air Force had been intensifying its operations. Gasoline and bombs were always in short supply but even so, the successors of the Flying Tigers were destroying 50,000 tons of Japanese shipping per month. With sufficient supplies and planes, Chennault had hoped that his force could be the agent for the aerial destruction of Japan. He had also maintained that his planes could thwart the Japanese land offensive in China if need be. One source of the conflict between Chennault and Stilwell was the latter's doubt about the value of air power against ground troops and his firm conviction that the Japanese would attack the east China bases of the Fourteenth Air Force if it became more than a nuisance. The new Allied strategy of February 1944 was to build up the Fourteenth Air Force to support the Pacific offensives against Japan, which explains the need to clear north Burma for supply purposes. With an improved flow of supplies coming over the hump in late 1943, Chennault then undertook an air offensive which swept the China coasts of Japanese shipping, thus severely interdicting Japanese sea communications with Southeast Asia. But Chennault was soon severely handicapped by a new shortage of supplies as he now had a competitor in China in Project Matterhorn.

The new and untried American super bomber – the B-29 – was sent to to China in early 1944 to fulfill the long cherished American ambition of bombing Japan from Chinese bases and as part of the political price paid to Chiang Kai-shek for his participation in the Burma campaign. This decision unwisely placed a voracious new consumer of supplies in a theater which had always been a logistic nightmare. Four B-29 bases were established around Chengtu and their defense given to the 312th Fighter Wing as its sole responsibility. This new operation ran the Fourteenth Air Force acutely short of gasoline in particular and indeed, the B-29s themselves were used to haul gasoline when not on tactical missions. Yet all told, the B-29s flew only twenty missions from Chengtu – nine to Japan, ten to Manchuria, and one to Formosa. The official American postwar assessment stated that these missions 'did little to hasten the Japanese surrender or justify the lavish expenditures poured out on their behalf through a fantastically uneconomic and barely workable supply system'. Wedemeyer finally prevailed on the Joint Chiefs of Staff to withdraw the last of the B-29s by January 1945. Only after the new bombers were flying from bases in the Marianas did the effective air bombardment of Japan really commence and the B-29 fulfill its potential.

Even before the B-29s arrived in China to menace Japan, however, the Fourteenth Air Force had in fact hurt the Japanese enough for them to undertake an offensive and thus fulfill Stilwell's prophecy. The last straw for the Japanese was a brilliant Fourteenth Air Force raid on the Shinchiku Airfield on Formosa on 25 November 1943. The success of this raid and the ease with which it had penetrated Japanese air defenses on Formosa demonstrated the necessity of destroying American air power in China. The subsequent presence of the B-29s was an added incentive. In December 1943 General Hata of the China Expeditionary Army ordered an immediate air offensive against American air installations to be followed by a massive army offensive against east China. As plans progressed, the scope of the offensive was enlarged to 'forestall the bombing of the homeland by American B-29s based at Kweilin and Liuchow' and to 'destroy the backbone of the Chinese army and force increased deterioration of the political regime'. It was also intended to establish a corridor between Manchuria/North China and Hanoi in French Indochina as an interior line of communication which would be relatively safe from air attack. The Fourteenth Air Force bases in East China were also to be eliminated. Code named 'Ichi-go', this offensive was the largest Japanese land operation of the war and ultimately involved 620,000 Japanese troops. If Ichi-go was successful, the next step was to be a drive up the Yangtze valley on the Chinese capital of Chungking, whose fall would have decisively taken China out of the war.

As the massive preparations for the offensive clearly indicated what was to come, the Allied forces in China found themselves in a desperate plight. Over 200,000 of the best troops were committed to the Burma campaign. Stock-piling for the B-29 project had left the Fourteenth Air Force generally short of supplies and acutely

LEFT: *US and Chinese troops operating together in northern Burma pick up supplies from an air drop.*

RIGHT: *Men of Merrill's Marauders on the march on a jungle road.*

BELOW: *Young Chinese welcome the first supply convoy to pass over the reopened Burma Road in November 1944.*

short of fuel at the threatened bases in East China; 200 of the 400 operational planes were also supporting the Burma campaign. Chennault was refused use of either the B-29s or the B-29 stockpiles and in April was even ordered to divert planes to the protection of a B-29 base at Chungking. Poorly led and equipped, the Chinese were incapable of halting the offensive, which began in April 1944, without the support of the Fourteenth Air Force.

The Japanese offensive rolled forward quickly and on 18 June took Changsha, a major rail center and gateway to the Fourteenth Air Force bases in east China. The drive then stalled for 49 days before the key city of Henyang, center of the Hankow-Hanoi axis. Despite the heroic defense put up by the Chinese General Hsueh Yueh, Henyang fell and by October the Manchuria-Hanoi corridor was completed. East China was isolated and the political prestige of Chiang's regime had suffered a disastrous blow. For the Japanese, Ichi-go had been a most satisfactory operation.

It was obvious that the crisis created by Ichi-go required that the Chinese troops in Burma and Yunnan be returned to defend China posthaste. The cargo planes of the hump run were initially used to transport the 25,000 men and 2200 horses of the Chinese Sixth Army to assist in the defense of Chihkiang, a key city controlling the approaches to Chungking. Organizing the defenses of Chungking Wedemeyer soon requested that most of the remaining Chinese troops in Burma be returned. Thus a further 25,000 well-equipped and battle-tested troops were airlifted to Chungking. These forces became the nucleus of a larger force organized by Wedemeyer to counter the expected renewal of the Japanese offensive. In April 1945 the Japanese did renew their attack on Chihkiang but, supported by the full might of the Fourteenth Air Force, the American-trained and equipped Chinese troops had decisively defeated the Japanese and caused the beginning of a general withdrawal by mid-May. Wedemeyer had shown what Stilwell had denied – that a coordinated ground and air defense could defeat a numerically superior enemy.

As a theater of operations, CBI was central neither to the Japanese nor to the Allies. The Japanese preferred to make peace rather than war in China, while both Chiang and the Allies believed that the war would be won elsewhere. The real function of China in the war was not to launch great offensives against Japan but simply to occupy the attention of over one million Japanese soldiers, soldiers who might have made a significant contribution to the defense of the Pacific had the leaders of the Japanese Army not been so enthralled with their China adventure. Burma was of marginal importance to the Japanese, serving mainly to protect the flank of Malaya and politically as a puppet state. The Americans thought Burma was important because through it lay the only line of land communication with China. The British concern with Burma stemmed partly from a desire to restore the military prestige lost in the débâcle of 1942, but mainly from a desire to restore their imperial position after the war.

8.
Iwo Jima

Iwo Jima is an island in the Bonin chain and is only four and one half miles long, and two and one quarter miles wide. It is nestled at the southern end of the chain which extends due south for 700 miles from the coast of Japan. The entire island is flat except for the rocky promontory of Mount Suribachi, an extinct volcano, which is 556 feet high on the southern portion of the island.

Iwo Jima was of great importance to the Japanese who used it for staging purposes on their routes to the central and southern Pacific. The early years of the war saw them build two airfields on it and after the fall of the Marshall Islands their importance grew. The conquest of the Marianas by the United States in July 1944 and their subsequent utilization for air attacks against the homeland even further enhanced the importance of Iwo Jima. It was more than evident that the Americans would need it for a staging point and advanced air base for the ultimate invasion of Japan.

The Japanese realized this and in early 1944 dispatched the 109th Division to the island. This unit was commanded by Lieutenant General Kuribayashi. He immediately strengthened all defenses, and began work on a third airfield in the north. Kuribayashi knew that the beaches could not be held and so he based his entire defensive strategy on a do-or-die effort around

RIGHT: *Marines are briefed on their target aboard a landing ship bound for Iwo Jima.*

BELOW: *Iwo Jima's airfields come under air attack in the lead up to the invasion.*

BELOW LEFT: *A group of Marines try to check a map reference for an enemy position so that they can call in artillery fire.*

Mount Suribachi and the Motoyama plateau. The US constantly bombarded the island but nonetheless, defensive positions were built in depth between No 1 and No 2 airfields, and between No 2 airfield and Motoyama, connected by a very intricate network of tunnels. These defenses were supported by heavy artillery and mortars conveniently situated in caves and camouflaged concrete emplacements. The same types of defenses were built around Mount Suribachi and, in addition, the beaches were heavily mined. By January 1945 the Iwo Jima garrison was over 21,000 strong and was waiting for the first Marines to land.

The reasoning behind the American decision to take the island was dictated by their policy of strategically bombing Japan into submission. As the Japanese High Command had realized, high losses of B-29 bombers on missions over Japan meant that the US had to ensure better fighter protection for bombers. The B-29s had been flying unescorted because none of the American fighters had the range to make the 2800-mile round trip between the Marianas and Japan. Iwo Jima was an excellent choice as an air base because it was only 660 nautical miles from

Tokyo and it had already been developed by the Japanese for that purpose. In fact aircraft on Iwo Jima were used to bomb the Marianas and it was necessary to knock it out as an airbase. The other calculation the American planners made was that since Iwo Jima was traditionally Japanese territory, its loss would a psychological blow to the Japanese people.

With all these considerations in mind, planning for the operation to take Iwo Jima had been initiated in September 1943. Following the fall of the Marianas Admiral Nimitz placed the entire operation in the capable hands of Admiral Raymond Spruance and his Fifth Fleet. The man in charge of the actual Joint Expeditionary Force was Vice-Admiral Kelly Turner. Vice-Admiral Marc Mitscher's fast carrier force was given the task of covering the main force. Spruance knew all about the heavy Japanese preparations so he arranged for the 7th USAAF to attack the island's defenses with B-24s from the Marianas. This continuous bombardment was to start on 31 January and continue until 15 February. Then a three-day naval bombardment was to begin. To create a diversion to pull away any Japanese air support for the island, Spruance ordered the complete complement of the fast carrier force to attack targets in the Tokyo area and airfields for the first time on 16 and 17 February.

The ground operations were placed in the hands of Lieutenant General Holland 'Howlin' Mad' Smith, who had been the commander of the operations in the Gilberts, Marshalls and Marianas. The invasion itself would be undertaken by Major General Harry Schmidt's V Amphibious Corps, which had amassed as much experience as Holland Smith of amphibious techniques. The V Amphibious Corps consisted of three divisions: the 3rd Marine Division, led by Major General Erskine; the 4th Marine Division, led by Major General Cates; and the 5th Marine Division, led by Major General Rockey, which was a new unit composed of a mixture of veterans and inexperienced troops.

The Amphibious Support Force arrived off Iwo Jima on 16 February and proceeded to soften the Japanese defenses. The Japanese, who had long expected the invasion, were convinced this was the main landing and opened fire with their heaviest artillery at 1100. The US had sent out frogmen to reconnoiter the shore emplacements and these men suffered over 170 casualties but they were able to bring back detailed reports on the Japanese defenses. Prior to D-Day these concealed coastal guns were extensively shelled.

On the morning of 19 February Turner arrived with the main force, some 450 vessels of

pinned down on the beaches. The weather, always a variable factor in amphibious landings, changed for the worse. Rising surf and extremely strong currents delayed the landing of reinforcements, tanks and stores of equipment. The Marines were hard pressed but as usual they plowed ahead.

The Japanese plan had been to wait for the Marines to get ashore and then open up. But 20 minutes after the initial landings when they had launched their artillery and mortars it was already too late as the Marines had brought ashore all the equipment they needed.

One specific action earned Sergeant Darrell Cole the Medal of Honor for conspicuous gallantry above and beyond the call of duty. While acting as leader of a machine-gun section of B Company, 1st Battalion, 23rd Marines, 4th Marine Division, Sergeant Cole was advancing with one squad of his section in the initial assault wave under heavy small arms, mortar and artillery fire, up the sloping beach toward No 1 airfield when he personally, at an extremely high risk to himself, destroyed with hand grenades two hostile emplacements which were endangering his unit's progress. Continuing to advance they were brought under tremendous enemy fire which succeeded in bringing their advance to a halt. Sergeant Cole set up one of his machine guns and managed to eliminate one of the enemy pillboxes which had his men pinned down. He quickly made an on-the-spot tactical judgement and armed only with a pistol and one hand grenade, advanced alone against the remaining two enemy pillboxes. He threw his hand grenade into the enemy pillbox, and returned for another grenade. He ran withering machine-gun fire from the enemy not once but three times before he succeeded in destroying all of the enemy positions. For this superb action under constant enemy fire, he was awarded the highest honor that a grateful country can bestow upon a hero. He was only one of 22 Medal-of-Honor winners at Iwo Jima.

By the evening of 19 February 30,000 Marines had been landed but the casualty rate was extremely high, more than 3000 dead. The Marines had eked out a beach-head only 1000 yards deep at the edge of No 1 airfield, and on the next day reached the west coast at the foot of Mount Suribachi. For the next three days the Marines fought to gain control of Mount Suribachi and finally at 1020 on 23 February a 40-man patrol was able to raise the Stars and Stripes on the summit. This feat was recorded in some of the most famous photographs of the war.

Spruance's Fifth Fleet was not left unmarked during the battle. On the night of 20/21

ABOVE: *The beach at Iwo Jima littered with casualties and destroyed equipment.*

LEFT: *Marine wiremen try to lay lines to a forward position under enemy fire on Iwo Jima.*

OVERLEAF: *Marines of the 5th Division begin to work inland from Iwo Jima's Red Beach.*

the Fifth Fleet. Directly after dawn the most concentrated pre-landing bombardment of the war was initiated by seven battleships, seven cruisers and numerous destroyers against the shore defenses. During this bombardment over 31,000 shells were fired, and in addition, the fast carrier force strafed the beaches, known defensive positions and camouflaged artillery for over 25 minutes. The first Marines were landing on the southeastern beaches by 0900 hours. Although the naval and air bombardments had been tremendous, the damage to defensive works had been minimal. Once the initial landings were accomplished the Japanese garrison erupted from its hidden caves and underground shelters, and the Marines were immediately

February 20 Japanese aircraft hit Mitscher's fast carrier force without inflicting much damage but the next day, the *Saratoga* was hit by five kamikazes, causing substantial damage. Only two hours later, another five attacked her but only one succeeded in reaching the ship. This time the damage was so extensive that the grand old lady had to return to the west coast for major repairs. On the same evening two more kamikazes attacked the escort carrier *Bismarck Sea* and within a couple of hours that ship went down. A reprisal raid against Japan was launched from the fast carrier force on 25 February but it was for the most part ineffective; immediately afterward bad weather set in. Mitscher then withdrew to his base at Ulithi. He did manage to make one parting strike against Okinawa on his way back.

On Iwo Jima the 4th and 5th Marine Divisions were fighting to gain control of the two northernmost airfields and on 25 February the 3rd Marine Division was brought in. The advance had stopped as the Marines had become enmeshed in the elaborate defensive network built by the Japanese. Artillery could not get at the underground positions and tanks could not negotiate the terrain. In fact Japanese and US casualty figures were evenly matched: it was merely a question of when the last Japanese would be killed. The final break-through did not come until 9 March when elements of the 3rd Marines reached the northeast shore of the island. The Japanese were finally isolated in a pocket near Kitano point and it was just a question of mopping up resistance. The Marines discovered the underground bunkers and caves which had protected the Japanese so well.

By 6 March P-51 Mustangs of the 7th USAAF were using the airfields on Iwo Jima and by April they were escorting B-29s to Japan. On 26 March 300 Japanese launched a final suicidal attack and Iwo Jima was finally under US control. It had been the most costly Pacific battle to date. Of the 23,000-man garrison defending the island only 1083 were taken prisoner. US casualties totaled 6812 killed and 19,189 wounded – almost 30 percent of the landing force. The Allied planners had underestimated the number of defenders on the island and had anticipated an easy operation. It turned out to be one of the most brutal operations of the war. With all the advantages the US had gained with control of the sea and superior air power, yet again the Japanese had proved an unpredictable opponent. The final tragedy was that Iwo Jima became just an emergency landing base for B-29s. Therefore the long and bitter struggle for Iwo Jima proved to be, to some extent, a useless exercise.

9.
Okinawa

Okinawa's strategic importance lay in its location. The island was the most heavily defended of the Ryukyu Islands and it was only 330 nautical miles from Formosa and 350 nautical miles from Kyushu, Japan. Once captured it would make an excellent airbase to step up the bombing of Japan. Okinawa could be used to train troops for the final assault on Japan and it also had the only two fleet anchorages available between Formosa and Kyushu.

Following the defeat at the Battle of Leyte Gulf the Japanese High Command was only too aware that the last battle was approaching. It was agreed that the final battle would be fought in Japan but also that the Ryukyus' defenses would be strengthened to delay the US invasion. After April 1944 Okinawa became a top priority for the Japanese and in August 1944 Lieutenant General Ushijima Mitsuri arrived to take charge of operations. Major General Cho Isamu was assigned to him and together they made a formidable team. Between June and August units from China, Manchuria and Japan were sent to Okinawa. These troops were in the main well trained but inexperienced and Cho, with his belief in iron discipline, prepared them for battle. The 9th Infantry Division had provided the backbone of the Okinawan defenses but the Japanese High Command decided to transfer them in December 1944 to the Philippines. They never made it to Luzon because of US control of the seas and spent the rest of the war in Formosa. Ushijima lost his best division which was never replaced; however he did receive massive supplies of ammunition and artillery. His defense force consisted of the 24th, 28th and 62nd Divisions, and the 44th Independent Mixed Division. By the time of the US invasion he had a force of 80,000 men, and of these 20,000 were native Okinawans. Ushijima decided early on that the doctrine of attack had been ineffective in

BIGGEST JAPANESE BATTLESHIP SUNK

Quarter Of Remaining Fleet Smashed

From DAVID DIVINE,
War Correspondent of "The Sunday Times"

ADM. NIMITZ'S H.Q., Saturday.

The Yamato, last of Japan's 45,000-ton, 16-inch gun battleships, and the most powerful unit in the Japanese fleet, has been sunk in a big sea-air battle with the American forces near Okinawa.

In addition, two Japanese cruisers and three destroyers were sunk and 391 Japanese planes were shot down.

An official Navy spokesman declared to-night that a good 25 per cent. of the major combat force left to Japan had been destroyed or put out of action in the battle, and that the whole of the Japanese fleet remaining "could be handled easily by any of our major task forces."

American losses were three destroyers and seven planes, with several more destroyers and some smaller craft damaged.

NEW JAPANESE CABINET

Premier Gloomy

NEW YORK, Saturday.

A Japanese News Agency broadcast reports that 77-year-old Adm. Suzuki has formed a Cabinet following the resignation of the Koiso Government 48 hours earlier. Suzuki will also hold the offices of Foreign Minister and Minister for Greater East Asia.

The new Cabinet consists of relatively unknown statesmen, and its members are a singularly unwarlike body. None of the great army figures who have been running the country for the past four years is included.

In his inaugural address the new Premier said: "The war, which is being fought for the very existence of our Empire, has come to its most important and crucial stage, and warrants not the least bit of optimism in our nation's survival. If the situation continues like this the basis of our nation's existence might be threatened. The enemy has now firmly established himself

According to a communiqué issued by Adm. Nimitz, the action began yesterday afternoon, when strong Japanese air forces attacked American ships operating off Okinawa and shore installations on the island.

It was in this action that the American losses were sustained. But no big ships were hit, and 341 of the attacking aircraft were destroyed—245 by carrier aircraft, 55 by fighters and 51 by anti-aircraft fire.

Early this morning, scout planes sighted the enemy naval force which had left the Inland Sea and, passing south of Kyushu, was entering the East China Sea. Immediately a fast carrier task force was sent to intercept it.

HIT BY 3 TORPEDOES

Carrier aircraft attacked about mid-day, in face of heavy anti-aircraft fire from the ships, but with no air opposition. The Yamato was hit by at least three torpedoes and eight heavy bombs, and sank about 50 miles south-west of Kyushu, the southern island of Japan.

In addition to the two cruisers and three destroyers sunk, three more destroyers were left burning.

Of the entire Japanese force, only three destroyers escaped, and they were heavily hit with rockets and machine-guns.

In other actions to-day, 30 Japanese planes were destroyed.

The Yamato, reputed to be of at

earlier operations and since his brief was to obtain the maximum delay he decided against attacking the US on the beaches and instead withdrew to the south, where he had a massive defense network built in the hills. The new slogan for the Japanese was 'One plane for one warship. One boat for one ship. One man for ten enemy. One man for one tank.'

The US assault on Okinawa had been planned for 1 March 1945 but it had to be postponed for a month because the operation on Iwo Jima had taken longer than planned. The US had assembled a force which was more than experienced. Although the Tenth Army as such had not taken part in any operations before, its units were veterans of campaigns throughout the Pacific. The commander of the Tenth Army was General Simon Bolivar Buckner, whose previous command had been in Alaska. The Tenth Army comprised the III Amphibious Corps, under Major General Roy Geiger, and the XXIV Corps, under Major General Courtney Hodges. The III Amphibious Corps was composed of the 1st and 6th Marine Divisions, which included men who had fought on Guadalcanal, New Georgia, Bougainville, Guam and Peleliu. The XXIV Corps was composed of the 7th Infantry

ABOVE: *The final instants of a kamikaze attack on a US warship.*

LEFT: *A kamikaze strikes home on the battleship* New Mexico.

ABOVE RIGHT: *Lookouts and a 'talker' aboard a US battleship off Okinawa. The talker's task was to give a commentary on incoming attacks to help direct the defending gunners.*

RIGHT: *Part of the massive armada assembled for the Okinawa invasion. Nearest the camera is the destroyer/ minelayer* Shannon.

Division and the 96th Infantry Division, whose units had fought in the Gilberts, Marshalls, Marianas and in the Philippines. Despite the fact that some of the men had been fighting for 30 months in the Pacific, all units underwent extensive training programs for the operations.

While the ground forces were engaged in training, Buckner's staff grappled with the logistical problems. The logistical plan for Okinawa was 'the most elaborate one of its kind developed during World War II, involving prearranged movement of both assault and cargo shipping over vast ocean distances.' The Naval Assault Force was similar to the one utilized against Iwo Jima. Vice-Admiral Raymond Spruance was in charge of the entire operation; Vice-Admiral Marc Mitscher commanded the fast carrier force; Vice-Admiral Richmond Kelly Turner commanded the Joint Expeditionary Force. There were numerous support groups: the Demonstration Group, commanded by Rear Admiral Jerrauld Wright, carried 2nd Marine Division; the Western Islands Attack Group, commanded by Rear Admiral Ingolf Kiland, carried the 77th Infantry Division; the Floating Reserve Group, commanded by Commodore McGovern, carried the 27th Infantry Group. The British Pacific Fleet also took part in the operation, under the command of Vice-Admiral Sir Bernard Rawlings. It comprised the battleships *King George V* and *Howe*, carriers *Indomitable*, *Victorious*, *Indefatigable* and *Illustrious*, the cruisers *Swiftsure*, *Black Prince*, *Argonaut*, *Euryalus* and *Gambia*, and 11 destroyers. The entire armada totaled 1450 ships of various types. The US plan was to take Kerama Retto on 26 March 1945 so that the naval units could have a protected anchorage for refueling and resupplying.

others in the Ryukyus of mines. An intense aerial and naval bombardment preceded the landing on Kerama. On 26 March at 0801 the first of four assault battalions hit their targets on the islands. By the end of the day units of the 77th Division controlled three islands and had established a foothold on two others. In fact shortly after the first landings the US troops had uncovered and destroyed more than 350 enemy suicide boats which would have been used against the main invasion force on Okinawa. Although Japanese troops were still resisting on 31 March the US forces had gained control of Kerama Retto for the loss of 31 men killed and another 81 injured.

The date chosen for the main assault on Okinawa was not only April Fool's Day it was also Easter Sunday. Under a blistering naval bombardment, an unopposed amphibious landing was accomplished on the Hagushi beach. Opposition was slight, and by early evening both Yon-

The III Amphibious Corps was to land north of Hagushi on Okinawa and the XXIV Corps south so that they could seize the Yontan and Kadena airfields.

From February onward US naval and aerial forces subjected Okinawa to intense bombardments. The Japanese responded by stepping up their kamikaze attacks so that by the time of the invasion there were very few aircraft left on Okinawa. The kamikaze attacks were aimed at knocking out the US carriers so that the aircraft from Kyushu and Sakishima Gunto could be used to defend Okinawa. Between 26-31 March some six US ships, including Spruance's flagship *Indianapolis* were put out of commission and at least ten other ships suffered much damage from kamikaze attacks. Nonetheless on 18 and 19 March the fast carrier force had attacked airfields in Kyushu and shipping in the Inland Sea as a preliminary 'softening up' process. The XXI Bomber Command in the Marianas was ordered to attack selected targets and various airfields in Kyushu between the 27-31 March, and in addition to mine the Shimonoseki Strait, the narrows between Kyushu and Honshu, through which the bulk of all Japanese shipping sailed.

Prior to the main landing on Okinawa the 77th Division landed on Kerama Retto on 26 March. Minesweepers moved in to clear that island and

ABOVE: *An Avenger opens its bomb doors at the start of its attack run over Okinawa. Note that this aircraft is also armed with rockets to complete its ground attack mission.*

TOP RIGHT: *An Avenger formation over southern Okinawa.*

RIGHT: *A formation of P-51 Mustangs in flight over Yontan airfield, Okinawa.*

tan and Kadena airfields were secured. Everything was 'looking good' and by 6 April the Tenth Army held the center of the island and could now pivot in either direction. The Marine Divisions had reached Nago at the base of the Motobu Peninsula, and both captured airfields were back in use. The first 72 hours of the invasion saw the Japanese 8th Air Division launch in excess of 80 aircraft to attack Allied shipping off Okinawa. The results were good: one destroyer, an escort carrier, two LSTs, one LCT sunk, two transports badly damaged, and another six vessels receiving minor damage.

The Japanese Combined Fleet commanded by Admiral Toyoda ordered a naval force consisting of the battleship *Yamato* under Vice-Admiral Ito, the light cruiser *Yahagi* and eight destroyers to sail from the Inland Sea and engage Allied shipping off Okinawa on 8 April. This final act of bravado on the part of the Imperial Navy was very reminiscent of the sinking of the *Prince of Wales* and *Repulse* because they too had lacked air cover. This force was sighted by a US submarine which relayed the important information to Mitscher. His aircraft located the enemy at 0822 hours on 7 April, 85 miles west of Kyushu. Two hundred and ninety-six aircraft were in the air and poised for the attack at 1000 hours. Meanwhile, Turner had placed a strong force of battleships, cruisers and destroyers across the path of the enemy force just in case it managed to elude or survive the massive air attack which was in process. By 1430 hours the power of the Imperial Navy in the western Pacific was most definitely at an end: the *Yamato* and *Yahagi* were both sunk, and four destroyers were sunk as well. The remaining four made it back to the Inland Sea but the end was now in sight.

Kamikaze attacks were increased on the Allied picket fleet off Okinawa. By 8 April the 6th Marine Division had secured the northern end of Okinawa and was beginning its drive into the Motobu peninsula. The Japanese were in strong defensive positions on the 1500-foot Yae Take hill. On 14 April the Marines came down on them like hot balls of fire, driving everything before them, so that by 19 April the entire peninsula was in the hands of the US Marines.

The Marines continued to mop up the northern portion of the island until they were redeployed in May to the south.

After clearing the northern part of Okinawa the next important target was Ie Shima, which lay northwest of the Motobu peninsula and was a large enough island to provide a useful air base. Again units of the 77th Division were used for the amphibious assault on 16 April. There was little opposition on landing but by mid-afternoon on 16 April the Japanese, concealed in caves and fortified tombs, were fighting for every inch of ground. There were more than 7000 Japanese troops on the island and they had converted Ie Shima into a fortress with an intricate maze of defenses. For six days the US fought in hand-to-hand conflict using bayonets and grenades until 21 April when resistance was finally overcome. Casualties in this operation were heavy: the Americans lost 239 killed, 879 wounded and 19 missing while the Japanese losses were 4709 killed and 149 captured. This struggle on Ie Shima would have remained unknown to the American public but for the tragic death of Ernest Pyle, the distinguished war correspondent. He died on the outskirts of Ie on 18 April.

The desperate attempts to stave off defeat on Okinawa continued. By 6 April Admiral Soemu Toyoda was ready to launch the first and largest co-ordinated kamikaze attack yet witnessed by the US forces. Fourteen planes were sent out to knock out the airfields on Okinawa but they achieved little but surface damage and did not knock out any aircraft. More than 100 fighters were then sent off to attack the fast carrier force and draw enemy fighters away from Okinawa. In all 699 planes (of which 355 were suicide sorties) were used in the attack on Okinawa between 6-7 April and they did cause much damage, including destroying all 81 mm mortar ammunition. A second mass kamikaze attack was mounted on 12-13 April this time using 392 aircraft and it achieved almost the same amount of damage. Most of the aircraft were flown by inexperienced pilots and carrier-based aircraft were therefore usually able to shoot them down before they reached their target. A third mass raid took place on 15-16 April and a fourth on 27-28 April and by this time US pilots had become expert at knocking them down.

On 9 April the XXIV Corps had come up against the Shuri defenses and since they could not make any headway General Hodges halted the advance and decided to mount an all-out offensive to knock the Japanese out with one blow. The offensive was planned for 19 April and during the four days preceding it the Japanese were subjected to intensive fire. Over 905 sorties were flown to soften up the Japanese positions. Also the firepower of six battleships, six cruisers and nine destroyers was directed against the Japanese line. The XXIV confidently expected to break through the Shuri line but soon after the attack was launched on 19 April it was apparent that the Japanese were so well dug-in that the US could make little impression. On 24 April the attack was renewed and this time made considerable ground because Ushijima had skillfully withdrawn from that line, unbeknown to the Americans. The US Army was not making the headway which had been expected of it and Lieutenant General Buckner redeployed the III Marine Amphibious Force, the 1st and 6th Marine Divisions, to take over the right flank from XXIV Corps which then moved over to the left flank.

Meanwhile the seemingly indestructible Japanese were suffering heavy losses and were beginning to lose ground. On 2 May at a conference at Shuri Castle the idea was mooted that it was time to mount an army-sized, all-out counterattack led by the 24th Division. Colonel Yahara Hiromichi, the operations officer of the Thirty-second Army, pointed out that the Japanese tactics had been successful up to now in that the US forces were suffering heavy casualties and that a counterattack was bound to fail given the numerical and material superiority of the Americans. His advice went unheeded and Ushijima decided to follow Cho's advice and mount a counterattack which took place at 0500 on 5 May. The Japanese offensive was well planned and co-ordinated with kamikaze attacks from Kyushu but failed to make any impact in the face of the intense US artillery barrage. By the evening Ushijima was forced to admit his mistake and issued an order to revert to the former tactics.

Buckner's reaction was to order an immediate renewal of a full-scale attack on the defenses of Shuri Castle, scheduled for 11 May. The American offensive against the Japanese line from the Asa river estuary to Yonbaru failed again and a contributing factor was the heavy rain which had turned the battle lines to mud. Wana Ridge and Sugar Loaf Hill were two of the main objectives.

Meanwhile the 1st Marine Division had been fighting under the guns of the Shuri hills. Here the 1st Division and the 77th Infantry Division encountered the Wana defenses, northwest of Shuri. Behind the Wana Ridge flowed the Asa River and the deep Wana Gorge. The Japanese had fortified Hill 55 overlooking the Gorge and the Marines had to take it. The 5th and 7th Marines moved against it from opposite sides. The 7th Marines, after five days of continuous heavy fighting to take the Ridge, lost 51 killed and 387 wounded in action. On 19 May the 1st Marines relieved them. The 1st Marines then immediately assaulted the ridge with grenades and heavy automatic weapons fire and succeeded in taking the crest. By 20 May the 5th Marines had managed to capture the western end of Hill 55 and were moving into the draw. But the Japanese still held 110 Meter Hill, and this made it virtually impossible for the Marines to advance on Shuri. Again the rains came and turned the entire island into a vast sea of mud through which absolutely nothing could move. By 28 May the rains had stopped and the advance began again. Tuesday, 29 May, witnessed the 1st Battalion, 5th Marines taking Shuri Castle. Okinawa was practically secured. So far, Lieutenant General Buckner's Army had sustained 5655 killed and 23,909 wounded in action, while the Japanese had lost over 62,000 dead.

Finally, fresh Marines arrived to bolster up the tired Assault Force; these were Colonel Clarence Walker's 8th Marines, 2nd Division. By the middle of June the Japanese defenses were weakening appreciably. Lieutenant General Buckner decided on 18 June to visit the front to see the 8th Marines go into action. He was witnessing the advance from the 3rd Battalion's observation post when an enemy shell struck nearby and blew a piece of coral into the general's chest. Buckner died soon after.

On that same day Ushijima issued his last order appointing an officer to continue the fight against the US as guerrilla warfare. Japanese soldiers for the first time were surrendering *en masse*. On 19 June 343 surrendered. On 21 June Ushijima prepared for ritual suicide and following a sumptuous banquet the Japanese general and his deputy, Cho, died in the early hours of 22 June. Although Buckner's temporary replacement, Major General Roy Geiger, was able to declare that Okinawa was secure on 21 June, fighting continued until the end of the month. The final official casualty figures for the 82-day campaign were excessively high: enemy losses were 107,539 counted dead, a further estimate of 23,764 assumed dead in caves or buried by the Japanese, and 10,755 soldiers who gave themselves up. These figures were estimated by the Tenth Army intelligence to include 42,000 civilians killed in the fighting by both sides. US losses amounted to 7374 killed, 31,807 wounded and 230 missing. There were also 26,221 non-battle casualties. These figures were a gloomy indication of the scale of casualties which might be incurred once the US invaded Japan.

The Americans had brought the war one step nearer to Japan and were now preparing for the greatest amphibious operation of all time – the invasion of Japan. They had brought the amphibious techniques of landing to new heights. As British observers commented 'this operation was the most audacious and complex enterprise which has yet been undertaken by the American Amphibious Forces . . . .'

RIGHT: *Admirals Nimitz (front left) and Spruance on an inspection trip to Okinawa.*

BELOW RIGHT: *The carrier* Bunker Hill *falls victim to a kamikaze on 11 May 1945.*

BELOW: *The comparatively peaceful scene on the Okinawa beaches arising from the Japanese decision only to begin their defense when the Americans had moved inland.*

10.
The Bombing
of Japan

In December 1940 Secretary of the Treasury, Henry Morgenthau, presented a rather strange proposal to President Roosevelt. Despite American neutrality in the Sino-Japanese war, it was suggested that a number of B-17 bombers should be given to the Chinese leader, Chiang Kai-shek, on the understanding that they would be used to attack Tokyo. Roosevelt gave his enthusiastic support, having watched with growing concern the Japanese air raids upon Chinese cities since 1937, and Chiang Kai-shek, understandably, was delighted. Unfortunately on 22 December General George Marshall, Chief of Staff of US Army, pointed out that there was a shortage of B-17s for his own air service and that none could be spared for the Chinese venture. Relunctantly, the plan was dropped.

Bearing this episode in mind, it might be imagined that the bombing of the Japanese homeland, with the familiar aims of destroying both civilian morale and the industrial base of the country, would have been initiated by the Americans immediately after Pearl Harbor. This was not the case. With the exception of a daring raid upon Tokyo by carrier-launched B-25 twin-engined bombers, led by Colonel James Doolittle on 18 April 1942, no American aircraft assaulted the air space of Japan until June 1944. It was not that Americans did not want to hit the enemy homeland but that, for a wide variety of reasons, they were incapable. The story of the campaign is a classic example of the practical problems confronting even the most sophisticated nation in the organization and conduct of strategic bombing, reinforcing the lessons of both the British and American offensives against Germany. Yet, ironically, the raids against Japan, culminating in those using atomic weapons in August 1945, probably came closer to vindicating the theories of people like Douhet and Mitchell than any others before or since.

Plans for a bombing campaign against Japan bubbled just beneath the surface of American

RIGHT: *A B-29 formation in flight.*

BELOW RIGHT: *The cavernous bomb bays of the Superfortress.*

BELOW: *The Japanese Army Kawasaki Ki-61 Type 3 (Tony, to the Allies) was one of the most important types used by the Japanese for home defense and was a fast and formidable opponent.*

strategy throughout 1942, but foundered on the first and most persistent problem – that of geography. With the massive expansion of her Empire in the aftermath of Pearl Harbor, Japan had created an extensive buffer zone around the home islands, leaving America in possession of no territory from which existing bombers could operate. A continuation of Doolittle's idea of using carriers was impractical, for even presuming that any could be spared, Japanese sea supremacy, particularly in home waters, was so secure that they would be extremely vulnerable. One possibility, suggested by Roosevelt himself, was the stationing of bombers in the eastern provinces of Russia, but Stalin, after lengthy prevarication, refused permission. This left only China – the area originally proposed in 1940 – but the practical problems were immense. To begin with, there was a complete lack of suitable

ABOVE: *An excellent impression of the massive size of the B-29 is given by this refuelling photo.*

ABOVE RIGHT: *Wrecked aircraft on a Japanese airfield after the surrender show the extent of the Allied superiority of the final months.*

RIGHT: *A similar scene of bomb damage and midget submarines in the dry dock at Kure.*

LEFT: *A Zero is the battered victim here.*

airfields and an apparently insuperable problem of supply, with no Chinese ports open to traffic and the Burma Road cut by advancing Japanese armies. In addition, even if air bases were constructed there was no guarantee that Chiang Kai-shek's troops could protect them for long enough to get a bombing campaign going. Finally – and this was the overriding problem – there was no aircraft in American service with the range to carry bombs from Central China to Japan – a trip of 1500 miles. Such considerations, coupled with the pressing need to stem the Japanese tide of victory in the Pacific, prevented the planning of a bombing campaign for the first 20 months of the Far Eastern war.

But Roosevelt never gave up the idea entirely. At the Casablanca Conference in January 1943 he discussed the possibility of bombing Japan with the British, and seven months later at Quebec finally decided, in the absence of any other remotely feasible option, to launch the raids from Central China. According to the President's arguments, the problems of supply and ground protection could be solved by basing the bombers in eastern India and merely refueling

them at special fields around Changsha on their journeys to and from Japan, while the question of range would be answered as soon as a new bomber, the Boeing B-29 Superfortress, became available. In theory it all sounded very straightforward, but in practice the problems were only just beginning.

The first of these concerned the B-29 itself. It owed its origins to the American air expansion of 1939, when Roosevelt, worried about events in Europe, had successfully pressed for the formation of a viable strategic bombing arm. The then Major General Henry Arnold, Chief of the Air Corps, immediately instigated an inquiry into long-term needs, and this concluded that a 'Very Long-Range' bomber was essential. A statement of desired characteristics was drafted and sent to leading aircraft manufacturers in America, asking for designs and contract bids. When these were received in May 1940, two were chosen for prototype construction, although it was apparent that the one from Boeing was potentially the winner. It was a radical design, contemplating an enormous machine with a wing span of 141 ft and a fuselage 93 ft long. It was expected to enjoy a

top speed of 382 mph at 25,000 ft, a range in excess of 7000 miles and a bomb-carrying capacity of 2000 lbs, the whole being protected by ten .50 inch machine guns and a 20 mm cannon in the tail. A wooden mock-up was ready for inspection by November 1940, and the air chiefs were so impressed that six months later, before the aircraft had even been test flown, an order for 250 was put in. Boeing built a completely new factory at Wichita, Kansas, and the first squadrons were confidently expected to be ready for service by late 1943. This deadline was never satisfied as delays in the development of the B-29 followed one upon the other.

The main difficulty arose because throughout the development phase the Boeing engineers were constantly breaking new technological ground. Their most persistent problem was weight. An aircraft of this size and potential was necessarily heavy to start with, but as new requirements arose from combat experience over Germany in 1942 and 1943, the addition of self-sealing fuel tanks and armor plating increased the weight considerably. Even after a special 'weight reduction board' had dispensed with such luxuries as soundproofing in the cabin and auxiliary crew bunks, the aircraft was still an incredible 105,000 lbs, without the addition of bombs. It clearly required extremely powerful engines just to get off the ground. Four Wright R-3350 18-cylinder, air-cooled power packs

ABOVE RIGHT: *A kamikaze pilot before his final flight to attack the Allied forces off Okinawa.*

RIGHT: *An Ohka suicide flying bomb being inspected after capture.*

Scenes of devastation after US air attacks. Tokyo (above) was the target of the most destructive raid of the war but the economy of effort involved in the one aircraft, one bomb, attack on Hiroshima (both left) signalled a new era in warfare.

were chosen, but they presented an entirely new range of problems. When the first prototype was eventually rolled out for testing in early September 1942 it was found that the engines were barely able to last an hour without burning up and, even after extensive modifications, it was engine failure which, on 18 February 1943, caused the second prototype to crash, killing the test pilot Eddie Allen and his entire crew of Boeing experts. This alone set the production program back by four or five months. At the same time other new design features were being constantly introduced, the most impressive of which was a novel type of armament system incorporating a small automatic computer which had the capability of correcting the guns for range, altitude, air speed and temperature, as well as a central control mechanism which enabled any gunner (except the man in the tail) to take over more than one of the five power-driven turrets. Such innovations necessitated more electrical power than the existing generators could pro-

vide, so 125 new electric motors had to be fitted to each aircraft. All this took time, until by spring 1943 it began to look as if the B-29 was never going to enter squadron service, let alone deliver bombs to Japan.

In an effort to speed the process up, the Army Air Force decided to take over the entire program itself, and on 18 April 1943 Arnold authorized the establishment of a 'B-29 Special Project' under Brigadier General Kenneth Wolfe. He was given responsibility for production, test-flights and crew training and, as commander of the newly-activated 58th Bombardment Wing, directed to prepare the B-29s for commitment to China by the end of the year. This was an impossible schedule, for by December 1943, although Wolfe was well ahead with a scheme to train 452 crews, each of 11 men, the aircraft were still not available. Only 67 of his pilots had even seen a B-29 and preliminary training was being carried out in B-17s. As a result, just before the Cairo Conference of that month, Arnold was forced to report that the bombing of Japan could not begin until mid-1944 – two and one half years after Pearl Harbor. Roosevelt was bitterly disappointed and did not disguise his anger, insisting that the first raid should be carried out no later than 1 May 1944.

But production problems at Boeing were not that easy to solve. By the beginning of 1944 only 97 B-29s had been built, and of these only 16 were flyable. The rest were at special conversion centers, undergoing yet another series of modifications. On 15 January Wolfe – now in control of 20th Bomber Command, of which the 58th Wing was only a part – had no aircraft at all ready for combat, and the new Presidential deadline looked as unattainable as the old. Once again, Arnold had to intervene, this time to sort out the troubles at the conversion centers. By taking personal charge of the whole process he managed, by force of personality, to get the planes moving at last, and in late March the first battle-worthy B-29 was handed over to Wolfe. By 15 April 150 were ready, being flown to India as soon as crews could be provided. The problems were by no means over – a number of bombers crashed *en route* because of over-heated engines, necessitating further delaying modifications – but by 8 May 148 had arrived in the Far Eastern theater. They were stationed originally at Kharagpur, Chakulia, Pairdoba and Dudhkundi in eastern India, but as early as 24 April a number flew 'over the hump' of the Himalayan foothills to the forward bases around Chengtu in Central China. Almost immediately, new problems emerged to delay the start of the offensive still further.

The first of these was supply, for despite a declared intention to make 20th Bomber Command completely self-sufficient, with its own transport element of C-46s, Wolfe soon found that he could not move sufficient stocks of fuel and bombs from India to Chengtu in time for a first raid on 1 May. Even when he stripped B-29s down and used them as transports, he was only able to deliver 1400 tons of supplies to the Chinese bases by that date, and of the 660,000 gallons of fuel needed, he had less than 400,000 on hand. He was forced to call upon the extremely hard-pressed Air Transport Command in the theater, but this brought him into conflict with local commanders, jealous of the official independence of the bombing squadrons. Consequently it was not until early June that a preliminary mission against railway stock at Bangkok could take place and not until 14 June that the first raid upon Japan could be launched.

Seventy-five bombers were briefed to attack the iron and steel works at Yawata on the island of Kyushu, which they did, but with depressing results. Seven B-29s aborted before leaving their bases because of mechanical trouble, four returned early for the same reason, three crashed on take off or landing and one came down in China. Of the remainder, 32 were forced to drop their bombs by radar because of cloud cover, 21 failed to locate the target and six jettisoned their loads indiscriminately. Little real damage was inflicted.

Nevertheless, Washington was impressed, and on 16 June Wolfe was directed to send his bombers 'the length and breadth of the Japanese Empire.' He was unable to oblige. Fuel stocks in China had been virtually exhausted by just one raid and logistical problems were so bad that it was impossible to build up supplies quickly. The Washington demand was unrealistic, and Wolfe said so. In early July he was recalled to America and replaced by Major General Curtis LeMay, a man of considerable experience, having commanded B-17 forces in Europe. He did not arrive until 29 August, and during the intervening period Wolfe's deputy, Brigadier General La Verne Saunders, continued as best he could. Kyushu was revisited by 15 B-29s on 7 July, fuel stocks were carefully restored, and on 9 and 10 August respectively, long-range attacks were made against steel works at Anshan in Manchuria and fuel plants at Palembang in Sumatra, the latter involving a stop-over at RAF bases in Ceylon. The results, however, continued to be poor and the Japanese began to react, destroying their

ABOVE: *The B-29 Enola Gay which carried out the Hiroshima attack seen here during preparations for the mission.*

RIGHT: *Colonel Paul Tibbets who piloted and commanded the Hiroshima attack. The aircraft was named by him after his mother.*

THE BOMBING OF JAPAN

first four B-29s on 20 August when Yawata was revisited. It was a very slow and unsatisfactory start to what should have been a 'decisive' campaign.

When LeMay arrived, he immediately introduced a series of new tactical ideas based upon his experiences in Europe. He insisted upon adherence to the prevailing B-17 doctrine of high-altitude, precision attacks in daylight, organized the B-29 squadrons into self-defending 'box' formations, and even borrowed the British technique of 'pathfinder' crews to lead the attack and mark a suitable aiming point. These innovations certainly improved the character of the bombing as well as crew morale, but did nothing to solve the basic problems of supply. All fuel and bombs had still to be flown from India to the Chinese bases – a journey of more than 1000 miles by air which actually consumed more gasoline than was being delivered – and this meant the raids upon Japan were spasmodic, lacking the concentrated force which was needed to make them effective. If long-term damage was to be inflicted, more convenient bases, situated in good supply areas and, ideally, closer to Japan, had to be found. This was realized as early as 1943, before the Chinese operations had ever begun, when Admiral Ernest King, US Chief of Naval Operations, recommended the seizure of the Mariana Islands 'at the earliest possible date, with the establishment of heavy bomber bases as the primary mission.' Full approval was granted at the Cairo Conference of December 1943, although time was clearly needed before the process could be fully effected. The Chengtu-based raids, despite their problems, had to be continued at least until the Marianas had been seized and airfields constructed. In the event, they were not phased out until early 1945 having, in the final analysis, achieved little beyond the gaining of invaluable experience.

As we have seen, the island of Saipan in the Marianas group was invaded on 15 June 1944 and secured by 9 July, with the neighboring islands of Guam and Tinian coming under American control a month later. Work on the airfields began as quickly as possible (in the case of Saipan while fighting for possession of the island was still going on) and the first B-29 landed on 12 October, bringing in the commander of the recently-activated 21st Bomber Command, (Brigadier General Hansell). By 22 November more than 100 of the bombers had arrived, enabling a series of 'shake-down' missions to be flown, chiefly against tactical targets on the islands of Truk and Iwo Jima. At first, the results were poor, with inaccurate bombing and

TOP LEFT: *J.R.
Oppenheimer,
scientific director of the
atom bomb project.*

unnecessary losses, but gradually things improved. By mid-November Hansell decided that the time was ripe for a raid on Tokyo – the first since Doolittle's visit two and one half years before. The attack was scheduled for the 17th, but the weather closed in, imposing a delay which lasted a week. The Marianas operations were beginning to bear a worrying resemblance to those from China.

This impression was reinforced as the new campaign eventually got under way. On 24 November 111 B-29s were briefed to attack the Nakajima aircraft plant at Musashi, Tokyo. Seventeen returned early with mechanical trouble, only 24 were able to pinpoint the target, six aborted the mission over Japan, dropping their bombs in the sea, one was shot down by fighters, one ditched in the Pacific on the return flight. The vast majority unloaded their bombs indiscriminately over the Japanese capital and, needless to say, the specified target was hardly touched. Nor was this an isolated incident, for the pattern was repeated in a number of similar raids and losses mounted steadily. By the end of the year it was apparent that drastic changes were required. The prevailing predilection for high altitude, precision attacks in daylight was clearly not producing the desired results: alternative tactics had to be found. As a first step in this direction, Hansell – a keen advocate of the discredited methods – was relieved on 1 January 1945 and replaced by the more experienced LeMay. He too was a believer in precision bombing, having been influenced by the theories of Billy Mitchell during the interwar period, so any new ideas had to be particularly convincing

to make him change his mind. Fortunately, the seeds of doubt had been sown during the last few weeks of his command in China.

The key raid in this process of change had taken place on 18 December 1944 against the Chinese city of Hankow on the Yangtze River, captured by the Japanese in 1938 and rapidly built up into an important military center. It was not a strategic target in the theoretical sense, and LeMay initially refused to contemplate it, but after specific orders from America he agreed to co-operate with the local air commander, Major General Claire Chennault, and commit his B-29s in their normal high-altitude role. Chennault opposed these tactics, however, persuading LeMay to send his bombers in comparatively low (18,000 instead of 25,000 ft), carrying incendiaries. The raid was an impressive success. Hankow was hit with over 500 tons of fire-producing bombs which gutted the docks, warehouse areas and surrounding sectors of the city. Some of the fires raged uncontrollably for three days.

The lesson was apparent: as Mitchell had pointed out as early as 1924, Far Eastern cities were highly susceptible to fire, being congested and constructed mainly of 'paper and wood or other flammable substitutes.' Precision bombing with high explosives was unnecessary and a waste of effort in such circumstances: area bombing with incendiaries would have a far greater and more immediate effect. The air leaders in America decided to try to switch as soon as news of the Hankow raid came in, issuing orders for test attacks to Hansell on 19 December. Incendiaries, including a newly-developed type containing napalm, which threw out

ABOVE: *The bomb dropped on Hiroshima was a Uranium fission weapon with an explosive yield roughly equivalent to 20,000 tons of TNT.*

ABOVE RIGHT: *An indication of the power of the bomb is this shadow left by its heat and blast.*

streams of fiercely burning petroleum jelly, were hurriedly shipped out to the Marianas and reports on their use eagerly awaited. But Hansell remained unconvinced – during the time when LeMay was *en route* from China he sent 57 incendiary-carrying B-29s to Nagoya (3 January 1945), but the results were inconclusive – and LeMay himself took some persuading. Only after heavy losses in precision attacks against Tokyo on 27 January did he agree – reluctantly – to switch to fire raids.

The first of the new-style attacks was carried out by 100 B-29s on 4 February against the city of Kobe. Sixty-nine aircraft located the target and results were good: an estimated 2,500,000 square feet of buildings were destroyed or damaged and local industry was clearly disrupted. LeMay was immediately ordered to elevate incendiary raids to top priority and given an extra wing of B-29s to make sure that maximum pressure could be exerted. Gradually, the new bombing philosophy took hold. On 25 February Tokyo was hit and one square mile of buildings destroyed, while on 4 March, on a return visit to the Nakajima plant at Musashi, the old idea of high altitude, precision attack received another blow when 159 B-29s inflicted minimal damage. In fact this particular plant became something of a test case, for after eight separate missions involving a total of 875 aircraft, little more than four percent damage could be discerned. Fire raids were obviously the answer.

Once convinced, LeMay characteristically devoted his full attention to the new idea, conceiving a major and dramatic change in tactics which involved removing all guns (except from the tail) from his B-29s, loading them up with as many incendiaries as they could carry, sending them at night to bomb the target from as low as 5000 ft, and guiding them in with special pathfinders. Tokyo was chosen as the target and the strike took place on the night 9/10 March. It was a spectacular success. A total of 279 B-29s, led by pathfinders, arrived over the city between 2400 hours and 0200 hours, high winds fanned the fires that were started and before very long the center of Tokyo was one vast sea of flame. About 16 square miles of buildings were completely leveled and the casualties were enormous. Over 100,000 people were killed, 40,000 injured and over a million made homeless, all for the cost of 14 B-29s destroyed.

Thereafter incendiary attacks were made on a sustained level and by the end of the Far Eastern war in August 1945 the statistics of destruction made terrifying reading. At first the major industrial and population centers of Japan – Tokyo, Nagoya, Kobe, Osaka, Yokohama and Kawasaki – were the primary targets, and by June a total of 105.6 square miles out of an aggregate 257 had been completely destroyed. Within these figures, the damage to individual cities was immense. On the night of 13/14 March 300 B-29s leveled eight square miles of Osaka, killing 13,135 people; two nights later 15,000 perished in Kobe; on 16 May 170,000 civilians in Nagoya were made homeless as four square miles of the city went up in flames; in two raids against Tokyo on 23 and 25 May, a further 18 square miles were devastated and the city temporarily paralyzed. B-29 losses were by no means light – between March and June well over

100 were destroyed on the fire-raids above – but the results could not be questioned.

Indeed, so impressive were they that by mid-June LeMay was able to report his primary targets destroyed and initiate a secondary campaign against 58 smaller Japanese cities with populations less than 200,000. Beginning on 17 June, when four low-altitude night attacks were launched against Kagoshima, Omuta, Hamamatsu and Yokkaichi, the process soon reached such a stage of sophistication that the B-29s were sent out on such raids every third day until the end of hostilities. This released them to carry out other campaigns against more specific targets such as oil refineries, merchant shipping and airfields, and there were even instances where a return to precision daylight attacks was both possible and effective. The main theme of the offensive remained, however, and the fire raids never lost their top priority rating.

By mid-1945 21st Bomber Command appeared to be the most devastating aerial weapon yet devised, but victory was not yet in sight. Despite the continued success of Allied offensives across the Pacific, Japanese resistance was fierce and heavy casualties were suffered by American, Australian, British and Canadian forces fighting under the commands of MacArthur and Nimitz. The appearance of kamikaze units and their accelerated use against Allied forces not only increased such casualties but had a psychological impact on Allied leaders and strategists far exceeding the toll that such units extracted in battle.

American concern with regard to the toll in life and limb which would have to be sacrificed in obtaining victory over Japan was clearly in evidence when Allied leaders met in Yalta in February 1945. Although the agenda of the Yalta Conference was hardly limited to a discussion of the situation in the Pacific and the Far East, this was a major topic. The American Joint Chiefs had made it abundantly clear to President Roosevelt that a Russian commitment to enter the war against Japan was not only desirable but necessary if a victory over the Japanese was to be achieved without the greatest bloodletting of the war. This argument seemed to be confirmed by the reports of the Battle for Iwo Jima which was taking place even as the Yalta summit was in progress.

The Soviets had made a vague commitment to join the war against Japan as early as 1943 but only after victory over Germany was achieved or appeared imminent. Faced with intelligence estimates that an Allied effort to attack and occupy Japan might cost as many as one million

casualties, Roosevelt and his advisors wished to have this vague commitment translated into reality and pressed hard to achieve this at Yalta. Stalin finally did agree to Soviet participation in the occupation of Japan but only on the condition that the Kuriles and southern Sakhalin be restored to Russia sovereignty and that Soviet commercial and strategic interests in Manchuria be recognized. For his part, Stalin promised to recognize the sovereignty of the Chinese Nationalists in Manchuria and to join in the war against Japan no later than three months after the surrender of Germany.

Although Roosevelt had succeeded in obtaining a pledge of Russian intervention against Japan, Allied military leaders were still concerned about the cost of final victory. Their concern and fear was heightened by the terrible bloodbaths on Iwo Jima and Okinawa where the price of victory was over 75,000 men. If the Japanese were willing to sacrifice more than twice these numbers in defense of Iwo Jima and Okinawa, what might one expect them to do in defense of their homeland? Not even the intervention of the Soviets served to allay the fears of Allied leaders. The specter of the occupation of Japan remained a bleak one.

Since Allied leaders were committed to the proposition of an unconditional victory over Japan, they chose not to respond to Japanese peace feelers made in April 1945. Rather, they continued to plan for the final victory over the Japanese Empire. In so doing, all efforts were

ABOVE: *The bomb 'Fat Man' which was dropped on Nagasaki. This was of a technically more advanced type than the Hiroshima bomb, being based on the element Plutonium.*

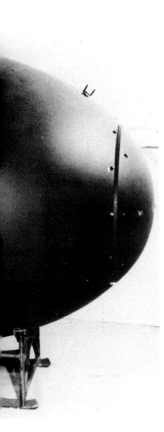

focused on achieving a final victory at the minimal possible cost, using whatever strategy and/or weaponry which might facilitate this victory. It was in this light that consideration of the use of the atomic weapon against the Japanese took place.

American and British scientists, assisted by refugees from Hitler's Germany and Mussolini's Italy, had long been laboring on development of the ultimate weapon – the atomic bomb. Although the race to develop atomic weapons had not been initiated with an eye toward using such weapons in the Pacific War, the fact was that the Manhattan Project was not completed until after the end of the European War. Indeed,

it was when President Truman was at the Potsdam Conference that American scientists informed Secretary of War Stimson that their 'ultimate weapon' was ready for use.

The availability of the atomic bomb injected a new element into the discussion of how to obtain the final victory over Japan. American military leaders were nearly unanimous in supporting the use of these new weapons against Japan if the war could be brought to a speedier conclusion than had been anticipated at the start of 1945 when Allied strategy called for an all-out attack on the Japanese Islands in 1946. Considering the horrendous battlefield casualties suffered on Iwo Jima and Okinawa, such a position was not hard

RIGHT: *The atomic mushroom rises over Nagasaki.*

to understand. On the other hand, there were those who opposed the use of this new weapon, arguing that victory could be obtained without unleashing a nuclear holocaust if Japanese peace feelers were responded to and if the Allies were willing to settle for less than unconditional surrender.

Debate over use of the atomic bomb against Japan continued from mid-April to 1 June 1945, at which time a special commission recommended use of the weapon to President Truman. Despite the protest and warnings of some of the men who had worked on the Manhattan Project, the President chose to accept the recommendation of his commission that the new weapon be used against Japan as opposed to some demonstration of its power elsewhere in the Pacific. He shared this view with Churchill in July. Writing after the war, Churchill summed up his reaction to Truman's revelation in a manner typical of the general reaction to this new opportunity: 'We seemed suddenly to have become possessed of a merciful abridgement of the slaughter in the Far East....To bring the war to an end, to avoid indefinite butchery, to give peace to the world, to lay a healing hand upon its people by a manifestation of overwhelming power at the cost of a few explosions, seemed, after all our toils and perils, a miracle of deliverance.'

While President Truman was discussing the atomic bomb with his advisors, Japanese leaders stepped up their effort to find a diplomatic solution to the war. The new government, headed by Admiral Suzuki Kantaro, a man who was privately known to favor an end to the war, attempted to ask the Soviet Ambassador in Tokyo to convey a message to his government in Moscow asking Stalin to mediate an end to the Pacific War. This effort followed a similar but short-lived attempt to have the Swedish government play a similar role. Although the Soviets seemed to show no particular enthusiasm for this suggestion, some Japanese leaders persisted in hoping that the Russians would carry their message to the other Allies. Other Japanese leaders steadfastly opposed this effort, preferring to fight to the death without surrender to Allied forces.

On 26 July 1945, even as Japan's frantic search for some way of effecting a cease-fire was in progress, Allied leaders issued the Potsdam Declaration which defined the terms under which the war might be ended. The Potsdam Declaration called for nothing less than an unconditional surrender of Japanese forces, an Allied occupation of Japan, and the dismantling of the Japanese Empire. For the Japanese, even those of a somewhat moderate persuasion, the terms

demanded by the Allies as the price for peace were unacceptable. Indeed, the Potsdam Declaration strengthened the hands of the hawks in Tokyo who wished to go down fighting and brought an end, at least for the moment, to further effort to find a diplomatic solution to the war.

Since the Imperial Japanese Government did not respond positively to the Potsdam Declaration, Allied leaders continued to prepare for the final strike against Japan. There seems to be little indication that the Soviets had passed along clear knowledge about the feeble effort of Suzuki to make peace but even if they had, it is doubtful that the Allies would have accepted anything less than an unconditional surrender from their foes. With their forces poised for the attack, the Soviets promising to join the fray, and the atom bomb ready for possible use against Japan, there appeared to be no reason to accept anything less than total victory.

After considerable discussion, President Truman approved plans to use atomic weapons against Japan.

Planning for such an eventuality had been going on for two years. Air Force chief General Arnold had been told of the bomb's potential existence as early as July 1943, when he was directed to modify B-29s as delivery platforms, a process which was completed, in the utmost secrecy, by the end of the year. Tests with dummy bombs were carried out at Muroc, California, in February 1944 and five months later a special combat unit was organized under the command of Colonel Paul Tibbets. Known as the 393rd Bombardment Squadron, it was part of a completely self-sufficient 509th Composite Wing which was to be based, again in secrecy, on the island of Tinian in the Marianas. The first of the modified B-29s left the United States in May 1945 and by July the entire wing was in place, ready to go. It was just in time. On 16 July the scientists responsible for the Manhattan Project successfully tested the first atomic device in the New Mexican desert, and the news was flashed to President Truman at the Potsdam Conference.

A mission directive was forwarded to Tibbets on 24 July, setting the first – and, it was hoped, the only – strike for 6 August against Hiroshima, with Kokura and Nagasaki as alternative targets in case of bad weather. Problems, for once, were few, however, and at 0245 hours on the specified morning Tibbets took off from Tinian in a B-29 nicknamed *Enola Gay*. He found the primary target in good visibility, dropping his bomb from high altitude at 0915 hours before banking

RIGHT: *The British battleship* Duke of York *during the surrender ceremonies in Tokyo Bay.*

OVERLEAF: *General MacArthur arrives in Japan before the surrender ceremony. MacArthur commanded the Allied occupation forces after the war.*

sharply away to escape the blast. Within minutes a tremendous explosion, equivalent to the conventional bomb loads of 2000 B-29s, had killed 78,000 people in Hiroshima and injured a further 51,000. It completely destroyed some 48,000 buildings, damaged another 22,000 and left 176,000 people homeless. The Japanese were stunned, but because of communication problems it took time for the government to react. By 8 August the Imperial Cabinet had still not met and the Americans began to doubt the inevitability of surrender. Truman authorized a second raid, using the only other atomic bomb in existence, and on the morning of 9 August Major Charles Sweeney set out in *Bock's Car*. His primary target was Kokura, but after three abortive bombing runs in poor weather, he switched to his secondary, alternative objective, Nagasaki. At 1100 hours he released his bomb, killing some 35,000 and injuring a further 60,000.

Speaking to the American public shortly after the first bomb was dropped, President Truman justified its use in the following manner:

'Having found the bomb, we have used it. We have used it against those who attacked us without warning at Pearl Harbor . . . .We have used it in order to shorten the agony of the war, in order to save thousands and thousands of Americans. We shall continue to use it until we completely destroy Japan's capacity to make war. Only a Japanese surrender will stop us.'

Although the atomic bombings of Hiroshima and Nagasaki had resulted in horrendous casualties, they had not resulted in a mentality of surrender in Tokyo. Although the Emperor's advisors understood the need to end the war, they were divided as to whether to accept the conditions for surrender described in the Potsdam Declaration or to fight on until such time as the Allies showed some sign of being willing to accept something less than unconditional surrender. As this question was being debated in Tokyo, the Soviets had entered the war.

On 8 August 1945 the Soviet Union declared war on Japan. One day later, on the day when the second atomic bomb was dropped on Nagasaki, Russian forces attacked in Manchuria, and overran the Japanese protectorate within less than two weeks. Ironically, the Soviet intervention, which Roosevelt had sought so vigorously at Yalta, came when it was no longer necessary from the American point of view. Indeed, many Americans, President Truman among them, viewed Russia's belated declaration of war against Japan with alarm, fearing that the Soviets would gain a foothold in East Asia from which it would be difficult to dislodge them. This was one of the reasons why Truman and his advisors appeared so eager to use the atomic bomb against Japan, hoping to secure a Japanese surrender before Russia entered the war.

The coincidence of the bombing of Nagasaki and the Soviet intervention in Manchuria forced the hand of the Japanese, causing Emperor Hirohito to break the deadlock between those who called for continued resistance to the Allies and those who called for peace at any price. At his urging, the Imperial Government sent a note to the Allies on 10 August 1945 calling for a cease-fire and subsequent peace talks. This note stated:

'The Japanese Government is ready to accept the terms enumerated in the joint declaration which was issued at Potsdam on 26 July 1945 . . . with the understanding that this declaration does not comprise any demand which prejudices the right of His Majesty as sovereign.'

On 11 August Allied leaders replied to the Japanese note, responding to their request that the Imperial institution be maintained as follows: 'The ultimate form of the government of Japan shall, in accordance with the Potsdam Declaration, be established by the freely expressed will of the Japanese people.'

Clearly, the Allied response contained no promise that Imperial prerogatives would continue to be recognized in the postwar period. Such being the case, die-hards within the Japanese government renewed their call for a fight to the finish, forcing Emperor Hirohito to intervene once again. At the risk of losing the very powers that made his intervention in the debate over acceptance of Allied terms for peace so important, Hirohito announced acceptance of an unconditional surrender to the Japanese people on 15 August:

'Despite the best that has been done by everyone, the war situation has developed not necessarily to Japan's advantage . . . In order to avoid further bloodshed, perhaps even the total extinction of human civilization, we shall have to endure the unendurable, to suffer the insufferable.'

On the following day, 16 August 1945, Japanese forces were instructed to lay down their arms and a new government was formed in Tokyo to prepare for the formal surrender.

Japan formally surrendered to the Allies on 2 September 1945. After almost nine years of being at war, Japan was at peace but the legacies of war were to be found everywhere. The country had been devastated by Allied air raids. Japan's urban centers were in shambles. In Tokyo alone, over 700,000 buildings had been

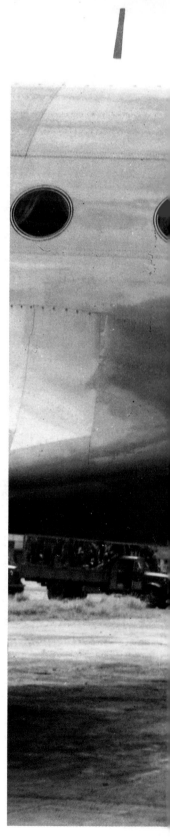

destroyed during the war and the population of the city had shrunk from 6.5 million at the start of the conflict in 1937 to approximately 3 million at the end of the war. Frightful as the physical destruction was, economic dislocation was even more alarming.

By 1945 the Japanese economy had totally broken down. Industrial productivity had fallen to one-third of that recorded in 1930 and worse still, agricultural output had similarly declined. Food was in such short supply that desperate city dwellers literally invaded the countryside in search of rice or paid exhorbitant sums to black marketeers to provide sustenance for their families. Prized possessions and family heirlooms were regularly bartered for food, and once such possessions were gone many had to resort to theft. However, despite this growing chaos, there were still those who opposed surrender. Fortunately, such people were in the minority

ABOVE: *Japanese officials sign the surrender documents watched by high-ranking Allied officers and the crew of the Missouri.*

LEFT: *Admiral Sir Bruce Fraser was the Commander in Chief of the British Pacific Fleet which joined the main US forces in the final months of the war. He signed the Japanese surrender on behalf of the British government.*

ABOVE: *General MacArthur looks on as the Soviet representative signs the surrender.*

and their sense of honor which led them to *hara kiri* eliminated many of the reactionaries from political life. Thus, when the Allied occupation of Japan was initiated, it did not encounter serious resistance.

The majority of the Japanese people accepted defeat and enemy occupation with a resignation and stoic acceptance that surprised their enemies. Unlike the Germans, who sought at almost all levels to place the blame for their predicament on others, the Japanese, whether of high or low station, did not seek to evade responsibility for what had happened between 1937 and 1945. Accepting the inevitable, the Japanese were able to cooperate with occupation forces.

When MacArthur's army of occupation arrived in Japan in the autumn of 1945, it encountered no overt resistance. To many of those in this occupation force, veterans of the bitter Pacific campaigns, the passivity with which the Japanese accepted the occupation seemed beyond belief. Conversely, the Japanese, who had been led to expect an orgy of carnage and rape in the wake of an Allied attack only weeks before the final surrender, were equally surprised at the discipline and order of the occupation forces. Within weeks after the end of hostilities, both sides were cooperating to rebuild the country and reshape her institutions.

Despite the fact that the occupation of Japan was an Allied effort, it was, in fact, an American show. Unlike the situation in Germany after the war, the occupation of Japan was an orderly affair with only one of the powers, the United States, dictating and directing the recovery effort. In no small way, this fact contributed to a reasonably amicable and trouble-free period of postwar adjustment, during which Japan, like the proverbial phoenix, rose from her own ashes. History provides us with few similar phenomena.

The Publisher would like to thank the following for their help in the preparation of this book: Adrian Hodgkins the designer, Ron Watson for the index, Veronica Price for production and Donald Sommerville the editor. The majority of the illustrations are from the Bison Picture Library and we are grateful to the following agencies for the remainder.

Imperial War Museum: pages 11 top, 13, 14 below, 15 right, 25, 26 top, 32, 41 all 3, 42 below, 43 top, 45, 67, 85 top, 133 below right, 135 below, 137 top, 138 below, 139 top, 140 both, 141, 144 both, 145 both, 146 both, 147, 148 both, 150 top, 160 top, 171 top, 175 below, 181 both, 185, 188.

Richard Natkiel: pages 38, 42 top, 46, 47 top, 70, 71 below, 105 top, 115 left, 119, 127, 138 top, 143 top, 164 top right.

National Archives: 68 below, 94, 96, 100, 108, 112, 115 right, 124, 126 top, 160 below, 169 below.

Navy Department: pages 12 below, 34-5, 50, 51, 53, 54, 56, 57, 58, 59 top, 62, 69, 79, 81, 89 both, 103 top, 106.